THE GREAT EXCHANGE

Experience Christ's Life by Letting Him Live Yours

Print ISBN: 978-1-936057-46-7
Kindle ISBN: 978-1-936057-47-4

Copyright © 2020 John Enslow

The Great Exchange

Experience Christ's Life by Letting Him Live Yours

Cover artwork by John Enslow
"The Great Exchange" Self Portrait, Original in Oil
Image Copyright © 2012, 2017 John Enslow

JohnEnslow.comNo part of this book may be reproduced or transmitted in any form or by any means, electronic or mechanical—including photocopying, recording, or by any information storage and retrieval system—without permission in written from the publisher.

Requests for permission should be made to: info@shulamite.com

Shulamite Ministries
P.O. Box 10
Suches, GA 30572
www.shulamite.com

Scripture quotations marked KJV are taken from the HOLY BIBLE, KING JAMES VERSION. Public Domain.

Scripture quotations marked NKJV are taken from the HOLY BIBLE, NEW KING JAMES VERSION. Copyright © 1982 by Thomas Nelson.

Scripture quotations marked NASB are taken from the HOLY BIBLE, NEW AMERICAN STANDARD BIBLE. Copyright © 1997 by the Lockman Foundation.

Scripture quotations marked ESV are taken from the HOLY BIBLE, ENGLISH STANDARD VERSION. Copyright © 2001 by Crossway Bibles.

Scripture quotations marked AMPC are taken from the HOLY BIBLE, AMPLIFIED BIBLE, CLASSIC VERSION. Copyright © 1954, 1958, 1962, 1964, 1965, 1987 by The Lockman Foundation.

Scripture quotations marked AMP are taken from the HOLY BIBLE, AMPLIFIED VERSION. Copyright © 2015 by The Lockman Foundation.

Scripture quotations marked HCSB are taken from the HOLY BIBLE, HOLMAN CHRISTIAN STANDARD BIBLE. Copyright © 1999, 2000, 2002, 2003, 2009 by Holman Bible Publishers.

Scripture quotations marked NLT are taken from the HOLY BIBLE, NEW LIVING TRANSLATION. Copyright © 1996, 2004, 2015 by Tyndale House Foundation.

Scripture quotations marked PHILLIPS are taken from THE NEW TESTAMENT IN MODERN ENGLISH BY J. B. PHILLIPS. Copyright © 1960, 1972 by J. B. Phillips.

Scripture quotations marked NIV are taken from the HOLY BIBLE, NEW INTERNATIONAL VERSION. Copyright © 1973, 1978, 1984, by Biblica, Inc.

Scripture quotations marked ASV are taken from the HOLY BIBLE, AMERICAN STANDARD VERSION. Public Domain.

Scripture quotations marked GNT are taken from the HOLY BIBLE, GOOD NEWS TRANSLATION. Copyright © 1992 by the American Bible Society.

Scripture quotations marked NRSV are taken from the HOLY BIBLE, NEW REVISED STANDARD VERSION BIBLE. Copyright © 1989, 1993 National Council of the Churches of Christ in the United States of America.

Scripture quotations marked TPT are taken from the HOLY BIBLE, THE PASSION TRANSLATION. Copyright © 2017. 2018 by Passion & Fire Ministries, Inc.

Scripture quotations marked CEB are taken from the HOLY BIBLE, COMMON ENGLISH BIBLE. Copyright © 2012 by Common English Bible.

Scripture quotations marked Moffatt are from the James Moffatt, A New Translation of the Bible, Containing the Old and New Testaments. New York: Doran, 1926. Revised edition, New York and London: Harper and Brothers, 1935. Reprinted, Grand Rapids: Kregel, 1995.

Scripture quotations marked RV are taken from the HOLY BIBLE, RECOVERY VERSION. Copyright © 2003 by Living Stream Ministry.

Scripture quotations marked BSB are taken from the HOLY BIBLE, BEREAN STUDY BIBLE. Copyright © 2016, 2018, 2019 by Bible Hub and Berean.Bible.

Statement of Faith

Providing a statement of faith has always seemed a little odd to me. As living epistles, our lives ARE our statements of faith. I live what I believe, and you should be able to look at my life and see what that is. This works perfectly in person, in churches, and in actual relationships. But when preparing to read someone's book, they aren't there in person and we need a quick reference to see if that author is playing for our team.

I don't think this needs to be complicated, so here is my very simple statement of faith:

Jesus Christ, the only begotten Son of God, came in the flesh, shed His Holy Blood on the Cross at Calvary for the sins of the world He is Lord of the universe, King of Kings, and I am His.

Table of Contents

Foreword

I was a young believer in my twenties. God had touched and captured my heart profoundly and I was full of zeal for Christ and hungry for the Bible.

Then my church invited a famous British preacher. Major Ian Thomas was an older man, He had been a decorated veteran in the second world war. He was famous in Europe for 'Torchbearers International,' his ministry of evangelism.

Major Thomas was full of a delighted joy that I had never seen before in any believer. He kind of sparkled!

Then came his message. It was strange and wonderful, very compelling. But there was one problem, I couldn't understand his meaning. I could hear his words, he knew something of God of which I had no concept. I was captured by the wonder of this strange truth he proclaimed, but for me it was all mystery.

Afterward I told a friend that I couldn't grasp his message. She replied, "Oh Martha, it's very simple." I answered her quite passionately. "Oh yes, I could teach it as a subject." And I put my hand over my heart and said, "But I don't have it here!"

I couldn't SEE it. I couldn't name it. I didn't possess it.

Yet I was deeply affected. For me, this was a mystery with a holy explanation and I wanted to unlock that secret. I was filled with hunger and longing for God.

So, I bought the Major's taped message and listened to it countless times. I could almost recite it along with him. All the time I was begging God to give me understanding! "Open my eyes, Lord and let me understand." To me it was a great and wonderful mystery of God and I wanted it with all my heart.

Through the tape message, slowly I began to see. The light came and I knew the name of the mystery. The name of the mystery was Jesus!

When next Major Thomas preached at church, I went to speak to him.

I was so excited, but all I could say was "I got it!" The Major had a little giggle when he was pleased.

He smiled down on me and correcting me a bit, in the way of that ever-present joy, he giggled and said, "You got HIM!" And He meant Jesus!

Yes, that was the mystery! I "had seen a revelation of Jesus." The exchanged life that Major Thomas lived before me with his piercing words and I discovered that Christ was **inside of me** as my very life. That He was *with me*, I well knew, but I did not know till then that Jesus was living in my body, to be everything for me, and for Himself. The wonder of it just left me breathless.

One of the Major's favorite words: "I vacate. He occupies."

I rode with the Major on the drive to the airport. I asked him, "In these 200 people, how many do you think understood your message?" I was so anxious for others to know this amazing truth! He smiled a bit and said, "Oh, one or two." He was content and seasoned in the reality of this knowledge – the understanding of this mystery had to be revealed from God Himself.

When John joined Shulamite Ministries at the age of 24, he had not been taught the 'exchanged life.' He had been taught "what to do to please God." And he was earnestly trying everything to do just that: please God.

As I began to speak about the 'exchanged life.' I said, "God is pleased only with the life of His Son and that Life lives within you."

"John, nothing in this will be about you, it will only be about Jesus."

I saw that John was crushed by these words and then - because he believed me – he was angry. He wanted to have a part in the works of "Christ" to make Jesus happy with him. He thought he had something to give to Christ.

That he had nothing to give the Lord, punctured all his hope.

In later years, we would often laugh about this conversation.

From that time, with the great zeal of the Spirit, John pursued the "indwelling life of Christ" as his one purpose. He began to grow in the exchanged life: his life in exchange for Christ's real Life living within.

In his passion for the God who performs His own will, John began an amazing journey and I was privileged to watch the "increase of Christ and the decrease of John Enslow."

John withheld nothing from God, as you will see from his story. He became a vessel only, willing for any assignment, accepting always the place of a servant, not for people's sake, nor his own fulfillment, but solely for the love of Jesus.

John's life exemplifies the unconditional love of Jesus, as a shepherd of real sheep and goats, including his infinitely patient care for the 'human Shulamite flock!'

John's life embodies Christ's servant heart, ever glad to take the lowest seat and the thankless task. By example, he encourages and inspires us all to join him in this extraordinary journey of the Exchanged Life.

He was growing in the intimacy of Christ living within. Along the way, some 25 years of living it, John wrote many insights and experiences of the *indwelling Lord.*

His lifelong passion for God, even as a child, is unique. But we can ask for that same zeal for God from the Holy Spirit. John's writing flows from submission to the Master . . . and to His presence dwelling within. John's great secret is that he lives by a close union with Jesus. His message was and is, ever this: "It's all about relationship."

John maintains a very private - often solitary life - with Christ. He seems to follow the pattern of Jesus, going aside 'to the mountains' to be much alone with God.

Watch for his writing about this bond of union with Christ. You will find that John places everything into that relationship with Jesus, everything issues out of that one companionship with the King.

One man, one pursuit, one companion . . . One God.

This book is the testimony of 'Christ's life' in John's life, as Christ: the real struggles, the divine chastening. It is not a story of John's greatness but of Christ's. He would say, a story of Christ's greatness in spite of John.

It has been 25 years since that conversation where John was eliminated from his own life. Those who know John in daily life, his church family, see Christ present and visible through his natural living.

To them - and to me - he is a hero of the Faith ,an UNTOLD story that can never be read in this world but will be celebrated in the next.

This writing is filled with insights, wisdom and deep knowledge of Jesus, lived through the surrender of everything and every moment to His beloved Lord.

This book is a miracle of John's personal transformation, who never thought himself capable to write a book about 'Who God is' and 'Who Christ is' and ''who the Bride is. There are more books to come.

John's journey is all about being reduced to *only a vessel* for Christ to express Himself.

You also have such a rich destiny, waiting for your passionate surrender to the Will of God. The will of God is John's one compass that has brought him to proclaim the Son of God with such personal revelation of God's mystery: Jesus.

This is a divine mystery, meant to be discovered, and open to be known.

The word "mystery" in Hebrew implies a "secret that is meant to be revealed."

to make God's message fully known, the mystery hidden for ages and generations but now revealed to His saints. God wanted to make known among the Gentiles the glorious wealth of this mystery, which is Christ in you, the hope of glory.
(Colossians 1: 25-27)

This book is God's invitation for you to see and experience Christ indwelling, the 'Exchanged Life."

—*Martha Kilpatrick*

A Vision of What is Possible

Christ wants you to be a vessel out of which His Life pours. It *is* possible (and intended) for your life to be fully Jesus, all the while being you. As a born-again new creation, you were not created to be a mere robot, unaffected by the passions of the Spirit. Whenever the Lord's Life and passion comes through me I am touched. He doesn't use me as a simple conduit, He purposes to involve me. But what God desires to produce in us is a life that reveals *His* words, His heart and emotions, without overshadowing them with our own. Doing so brings Jesus Christ and *His* Word into our world, and *His* Life is reproduced in others. Not more information or methods but a living impartation, Life begetting Life.

Imagine witnessing Christ's Life NOW! Yes, we are given the privilege to walk with Him, just as if we were walking with Him physically on this earth. But beyond simply observing Jesus' earthly steps as His original disciples did, today we can have Him walk every step ***in*** our lives. This is beyond being a spectator; this is bringing heaven to earth. Jesus brings me into Life, by being my very life. *This is the Great Exchange, the mystery of the Gospel, given to us as God's greatest gift.*

Introduction

Absolutely **DO NOT** read this book if you want to remain the same. If you like where you are and are satisfied with your path, then please grab another book. Or if you are just looking to collect another merit badge for your *good* Christian life, **PLEASE, PLEASE** do not read this book! To hear about **Christ's Life as your life will disappoint you greatly and make you utterly miserable.** But if you are done with the status quo and want to experience true, lasting victory, please continue. The revelation in this book has the potential to change everything for you, forever. This is not hyperbole; this is a living fact. To embark on the journey revealed in these pages will radically alter the landscape of your life.

You might ask me, "John, What are your qualifications to write a book on the exchanged Life? How do you know *anything* about this great mystery of 'Christ in you, the hope of glory'?"

My answer is simple. I have learned that those who have the *most* to say about a subject are themselves the original intended pupil for the lesson. I have much to say about the exchanged Life because I have had so much need to learn about it. The Lord has been pouring out His revelation on me, not because I am so knowledgeable *but because I am so needy.* I need this lesson more than any. My qualification to write a book on the exchanged Life has been earned through necessity. I have become an expert out of sheer desperation, not sufficiency, and *that* is precisely the point.

In writing this book I have deeply questioned myself: "Do I possess the exchanged Life? Is it made evident in my daily reality? Does Christ's Life face my struggles? Is my life truly 'Christ in me' rather than just *me*?" The answer to all these questions is the same. The exchanged Life is not a possession to be had, it is the Person of Christ.

So it is not that I have *it*, it is that Jesus has me. The exchanged Life is not a possession to be acquired; rather, we become His possession. Our life is His Life.

You might also ask, "Will I feel it when Jesus is living my life? Am I aware of the flow of His Life?" Not necessarily. Christ's Life as my life is a mystery. The working out of 'not I but Christ' will be as unique to you as your fingerprint. It is wonderful! Yet how can it be Him and not me, while it is still totally me? Read on to find out!

I not only give the scriptural basis of the exchanged Life in these pages, I also share deeply personal examples of how He has been Christ in *me*, my hope of glory. You will see what it looks like in an actual life. This is what always amazed me about Christ's Life on this earth. He revealed principles, shared truths, and then made them evident through His Life. It was not just an anointed sermon; it was a display of the Living God. This is what it is to live 'not I but Christ.'

Come read *The Great Exchange* and allow the distinction between you and Christ to be abolished. Become a witness to the most fascinating Life known to man, as Jesus lives His Life through you. Watch as He solves all your life quandaries, becoming the very solution you have so longed to receive. Impact your world with the Life of the Son and see Him perform His miracles in those around you. This message has the potential to be the last message you will ever need. Do you dare continue? I hope so!

What Stands Between Me and The Great Exchange?

Christians are continually trying to *change* their lives; but God is calling us to experience the *exchanged* life. Christianity is not a self-improvement program. It isn't a reformation project. It is resurrection! It is new life! And it is expressed in terms of a total exchange of identity.

Bob George
(Bible Teacher 1933-2018)

My Humanity Does Not Get Me There

Here is a truth that can shoot us into the stratosphere: **We are each a vessel made of clay to contain – *not produce* – the passion and pleasure of God.** This is great news, but it can also seem like a limitation of our very creation. "Doesn't *my* life make God happy? I am only a container? How insulting!"

Have you felt the burn of **God's** desire? I know you probably have, but did you know this was what you were experiencing? I did not. I thought that I was begging and pleading to be with the Lord from a desire that originated from me. Ha! What godly passion can dust and spittle manufacture of its own accord? Have you ever seen mud desire? Have you ever seen clay, a hunk of nothing, with eagerness for anything? No, we see it lying there like a lump. It can be resistant on a potter's wheel if not moist enough, but possessing godly passion? No, if enthusiasm for God emanates from us, it is safe to say that it has been breathed into us from an outer, nobler Source.

These yearnings and cravings for the Lord are but His own desire flowing through us. If I believe that my desire for God is *from* me and not His desire flowing *through* me, then I will become disillusioned, discontented and eventually embittered, because my human view is that I want Him and He is not coming to meet my need. But let's see it another way: What if God is upping the ante for His desires to be revealed in me? What if He is setting us up to go beyond our current level of desire to experience *even more* of Himself?

One morning I began my quiet time as I normally do, saying "Oh God, please speak to me! Please express Yourself to me today!" His reply that day was, "I AM pouring." At first I thought, "Was that thought mine?" But I realized that God was speaking to me. He was saying, *"I am pouring within you My own desire. I am filling you to the brim with passion for Me. Yes,* ***My*** *passion. I am going to drink deep, but now I am pouring from My pitcher into you, My cup."*

You and I are God's cup! Clay-made vessels to receive Him. Impassioned by Him, the desire of our life. If you have yearnings for the Lord, passions unsatisfied which seem to be turning stale, take heart! The continued longing is not a ploy to frustrate you. It is not an abuse perpetrated by a neglectful God. No, it just might be His pouring into you. I do not want Him only to sip, a quick connection and then pass by. No, I want to wait for God to pour in as much as He wants to pour, so that He can drink from me as much as He wants to drink.

Though the times of waiting may seem like an eternity, it is just a season. He is worth the wait, no matter how our flesh and soul may try to persuade us differently. Waiting is a willingness to be still in His presence as He fills us full. We wait until every last drop has been poured in, then when God is satisfied, we will be, too. We will be a vessel to bring pleasure to the Eternal King, and this communion will make our joy complete.

Houston, We Have a Problem!

As a vessel created to contain the Spirit of Christ, have you renounced your life? I have! What do I mean by this? I renounced my struggle to be the *source* of my life. In my struggles to live this life on my own, I only prolonged my pain and failure, as well as inflicting pain on others. The reason is because flesh is putrid! At my best, I'm still malignant. My highest expression of human effort is still just earthly, temporal, and more likely than not, destructive. The result of living life in SELF is depression and defeat. But here is an interesting surprise. We are all anointed failures. ***Anointed?!*** Yes, our flesh is ordained to fail.

The only valuable Life lived in my form and frame is the resurrected life of Christ—His Life, not mine. On my own, I'm like an open grave, just a dark hole in the earth. But as Christ emanates from my earthen vessel, so does His resurrected Life. Just as He rose from the tomb before ascending to the Father, now He emerges from within me to BE LIFE. Christ's Life, in my life, is the Father's Power and Purpose on the earth. It's only when Christ's Life is my life, that there is eternal value and supreme expression. His Life is heavenly!

When Christ walked this earth, He did nothing that did not originate from the Father. He performed *no task* on this earth from His own will. So Jesus explained, *"I tell you the truth, the Son can do nothing by Himself"* (John 5:19). Jesus and the Father were one; there was no independent expression in any of Christ's actions. This being the case, why would Jesus now expect me to do what He Himself was unwilling to do? Does He ask me to wield this deadly weapon of self-expression? No, He does not!

Here is the good news. Adam's failure was a success! The Father was not thrown off His game by man's fall. He did not scurry about looking for "plan B" after Eden. All of mankind *had* to crash. We were ordained to do so in order that the Life of the Son could come forth through us. Adam had to fail so that Christ might be glorified as the *only* Life that pleased the Father. We, too, are successful failures. We are called to fail, because we can do nothing other than fail on our own. But failure is an invitation to let Jesus succeed. Our failures lead to Christ's victory.

> *"My grace is sufficient for you, for My strength is made perfect in weakness." Therefore most gladly I will rather boast in my infirmities, that the power of Christ may rest upon me. Therefore I take pleasure in infirmities, in reproaches, in needs, in persecutions, in distresses, for Christ's sake. For when I am weak, then I am strong.*
> *2 Corinthians 12:9-10 NKJV*

If we could perform this life in our own strength, what need would we have of God? I certainly would not humbly come and ask for His Life in exchange for my death. I'd walk up to the front of the stage and pick up my gold medal. You would get a chance to see it, because I would show everyone on this earth. That would be my sole job – polishing my medal and touring around to show it to YOU! But that is not the prize we are to get. Our prize is that Christ has chosen to use us to bring forth His Life. **We are vessels made of clay to *contain*, not produce, the passion and pleasure of God.**

If you know you are a huge failure, if you have done everything wrong, if your list of defeats buries you beneath a weight of shame, then renounce your life alongside me. Let Christ rise from the pile of your ashes and live a Life that is eternal, impactful, and pleasing to the Father. Whether you have 5 minutes, 5 years, or 50 years, left to let His Life shine, Jesus can and will bring forth the Will of the Father through you and impact your world for eternity.

And my present life is not that of the old "I", but the living Christ within me. The bodily life I now live, I live believing in the Son of God, who loved me and sacrificed Himself for me.
Galatians 2:20 Phillips

Receiving the Reality of ME

Now that I have renounced my life for His Life, do I get to escape it? No, even with Christ's Life being my life, I still have to do a work of accepting the story He has set forth as my life. I am not unscathed by my choices, I have to do a work of acceptance.

For years I have worked to accept my life in its entirety. I have wanted to receive the good, the bad, and the ugly. It is *my* story and the only one I will ever have. It is not natural for us to embrace our story, no matter how terrific or terrible—by nature, we are just a discontented bunch. We simply do not accept the story God has given to us, nor appreciate walking it out before the world with all its foibles and blunders. This is mankind!

This all said, I do know the incredible value of accepting our stories. In Martha Kilpatrick's booklet, *The Great Lie,* she says,

> *"God explained that 'making peace' means:*
> *'**Accept, accept, accept** the life I have given you. Desire no other life. When you receive the life I have given you, I will **show** you the life that I have given you.*
> *'Deep, deep submission in your own being to your own existence – your own **brutal being** – to the limits of who you are and the limitations of who you are not.'"*[1]

These are simply amazing words! And I have purposed to do exactly this. But it is not an easy work. Most of us prefer to blink out the parts or aspects of our lives we just do not like, or even indulge in revising our history. To actually accept the raw truth of our story, in all its brutal honesty, is a courageous task indeed. We have been abused and mistreated, yes, but we have also been foolish, willful, rebellious, and even stupid. It is easier to receive the peaks of my life and ignore the valleys, but that is not the truth.

I am not talking about a "tabloid TV show" revealing myself to the world. This is a deeply personal work of acceptance in my heart. It is receiving God's authoring in order to see His handiwork. And without embracing His story of me, I will not see the beauty of His masterful craftsmanship.

Did He not know that my circumstances would inevitably lead me to trek down certain paths? Of course! No, He did not cause me to sin, but He also did not prevent the alignment of situations that made it possible for me to fall down. Although He's saved me from countless catastrophes, God did not eradicate every source of stumbling. Christ chose me to contain His very Life, and I must accept the vessel in which He chose to dwell. Imagine, I can reject the life God Himself chose to indwell just because I do not like the vessel! You can't reject the vessel and accept His Life within that vessel.

For we are God's masterpiece. He has created us anew in Christ Jesus, so we can do the good things He planned for us long ago.
Ephesians 2:10 NLT

Being True to Myself

It is not enough to accept the life we THINK God has given us. We also have to accept the life He REVEALS to us. And that only happens when we embrace the truth.

"To thine own self be true."

This phrase from Shakespeare's *Hamlet* is such a dynamic human truth. There are two ways of being true to ourselves: knowing who we are in the natural self, and knowing who we are in Christ. Both are so vital.

The deep spiritual work of knowing ourselves in the natural must be done in perfect honesty as the Spirit reveals it to us. The Spirit comes to show us our **brutal being** and we have to own it. As He shows us who we are in our sinful nature, we must say, "Yes, God, this is true. I am exactly what You say!" To reject it is to call God a liar—a foolish path because He is coming to set us free. It is a deep work of acceptance where we need much forgiveness. To own my wretchedness is a transforming work of the cross. Part of the work of salvation is coming to know why I need a Savior. "To thine own self be true."

The Spirit also reveals who I am in Christ. This can be equally as difficult to accept, especially if you're a neurotic. I know my wretchedness but to receive the truth of who Christ is in me is quite another thing. In reality however, it is just as evil to fail to listen to the Spirit about this as it is to refuse His assessment of my sinful human condition.

Knowing who we are in Christ is a *must*. It is how Jesus reveals His life through us. **Christ in me is His Life through me and to this I must be true.** His envisioned life in us is His perfect will for us.

We experience His Life living through us only inside of His Will. So, *"to thine own self be true"* is being true to the reality of who we are apart from Jesus Christ, as well as believing *His* idea of our New Creation.

It is Not too Big for Jesus

When you have seen yourself in God's Holy Light of truth and accepted it, what happens next? A miracle! It is undeniable that Christ performed many miracles. He cleansed the lepers, raised the dead, and delivered the demonically tormented. Wherever Jesus went, He made the wounded whole, cured diseases and healed sickness. Without a doubt, He set the captives free. Jesus was Kingdom liberation, and freedom followed in His wake.

Many of us know that He still performs miracles. Yet how many of us actually see these miracles performed in our most desperate places? Think about the areas that you struggle with the most. The area you would consider to be your place of highest need. This is obviously deeply personal. So, has He visited you there, in your private crises, whatever they may be?

Christ wants to come and reveal His Life and purpose in our deepest shame. He wants to reveal Himself in our deepest crisis, bringing life to our dead area, healing our leprous place. Whatever the malady, Christ wants to be known *there* as triumphant.

All of us came to Jesus with some form of death—whether it was "good" leprosy, evil leprosy or carnal leprosy, we came with death. He called each of us while we were still in an unclean state. And He specifically called us in our sinfulness so that He could be revealed as King over and through that very sinfulness!

Let's say you were religiously evil. Christ wants to reveal to you, *in* that religious evil, that He can overcome it. He wants to be RIGHTEOUSNESS in the face of your religious evil. Or perhaps you were a carnal sinner. Christ wants to live His RIGHTEOUSNESS in that place void of purity. Christ's own Life enters the very place of my death, whatever that looks like.

Name your worst and lowest. That is where Jesus wants to be Christ. He wants to personally display His victory over it, *in you*. We are given front row seats to witness His victory over our depravity.

Too many of us dwell in the shame of our condition, which keeps us from His Life. The closed fist of shame cannot experience His liberating freedom. Shame holds onto sin, while surrender releases it *to Him*. We have to open ourselves to Jesus in that place of shame, so He can show Himself to us.

Your besetting sins are used to reveal Christ's victory over *you*. Only you can possibly understand the magnitude of a victory so intimate and unique. Jesus does not care what the sin is; when we are His, it is our living assignment to witness Him as Victor over it.

Our individual sinful conditions are but an invitation for Him to enter in to reveal Himself in His Life as bigger than, and able to overcome, whatever sin boasts of its power. These things that seem insurmountable, much too big to conquer, are set up to display *His* power—a personally handcrafted demonstration of His Life.

This takes the sting from our besetting sins. We hand it to the Lord of Life, who brings resurrection out of death and beauty from the ashes.

But the Law came to increase and expand [the awareness of] the trespass [by defining and unmasking sin]. But where sin increased, [God's remarkable, gracious gift of] grace [His unmerited favor] has surpassed it and increased all the more…

Romans 5:20 AMP

Facing it ALL, with Christ

Do not let the truth of your brutal being lead you to shame, as it did to Adam and Eve. Sin makes us ashamed and tempts us to hide. And this is Satan's hope – our separation from God.

Which one of us does not wish to clean up their mess before anyone sees it? We feel it is better to fix it rather than get caught and be punished. This is the nature of sin. Sin perpetuates fear, and in that fear, we hide rather than seek help. Pride, lust, entitlement, and envy are all sins that separate us from God. This is why Jesus desires us to *involve* Him, not *exclude* Him. He says, "Bring Me into it. Let Me face it with you, as you!"

This strikes against the ploy of Satan. To face our sin in Christ exposes us to His healing Light and opens our hearts to Him as the Source of Life. I was never called to struggle and strain against my sins through self-effort.

The enemy knows as long as we are continually attempting to overcome our sinful self apart from Christ, we are separating ourselves from the Overcomer. Then guilt weighs on our hearts, which shames us further and pushes us away from God. It is like a fireman attempting to put out a forest fire without water or hoses. All the spit and stomping in the world fails to put out the flame.

The scheme of the devil is designed to divert our union and fellowship with Jesus. As long as I am exerting myself to do the work of *being* Christ, then *I am the christ,* not Jesus. Utterly frightening!

I'm not meant to be alone, conjuring my own righteousness. I allow Christ's righteousness to be righteous in me. Bringing Jesus into it unveils the separating lie which keeps us on the devil's treadmill.

Then we embrace the reality that relationship with Christ is in everything and everywhere.

Jesus lives ALL of life through me *as me* from my basest struggle to the most spiritual mountaintop. His Life is not to be compartmentalized into spiritual and secular, or natural and divine. Christ is my Life and He is with me in everything.

"But if Christ is in you, though the body is dead because of sin,
the spirit is life because of righteousness."
Romans 8:10 NRSV

"Because the God who said, Out of darkness light shall shine,
is the One who shined in our hearts to illuminate
the knowledge of the glory of God in the face of Jesus Christ.
But we have this treasure in earthen vessels
that the excellency of the power may be
of God and not out of us."
2 Corinthians 4:6-7

I'm NOT Called to Fix It

Jesus Christ desires to face our sin *with* us in relationship, rather than us trying to fix ourselves alone. Too many work to overcome their sins rather than letting the Overcomer conquer within them. This is just hiding your sin rather than dealing with it. Hiding it only keeps the sin alive, while we are to live dead. And to live dead, we must live *in Christ*. When we live striving and laboring, we are very much alive. It is *our effort* rather than *Christ's Life*.

In her *Fear Not, No Fear* audio series, Martha Kilpatrick says that any fear is the evidence of idolatry and unbelief. So, in this scenario of fixing or hiding sins, what is the idolatry? Self. And sin.

When I hide my sin in fear, I am in idolatry of the very sin I am trying to repair. Yes, the sin I am trying to conquer through effort rather than Christ's life is now my idol. Oh Jesus, have mercy on us!

Christ is committed to be involved in our lives. Jesus is Immanuel, 'God with us.' His involvement is not that of a fair-weather friend. It is ALL of my life—the good, the bad, and the ugly.

Satan tempts us to hide our areas of lack and sin, but it is in this area of sin that Christ, too, desires to dwell. Jesus' Life permeates through *our whole story*. Once we are His, He owns our past, present, and future. He's to be our New Creation and to overcome our old nature. Preventing His access to any area of my life is assurance of my failure, even if I am trying to overcome it.

Life is impossible if it is managed and manhandled by us. For over the millennia man has attempted to "be" what only God can Be. The struggle has depressed, angered, and frustrated all humanity.

All our endeavors to resolve the fallen nature apart from Christ's own Life have proved to be an inevitable failure. We cannot rule over our old nature; we can only surrender to His New Creation. The New Creation is Christ in me. Jesus' Life and sacrifice is the only way to satisfy the Father.

Christ resolved my besetting sin on the cross. Bitterness is not solved through my attempts to not be bitter. Bitterness *was* forgiven and Christ reveals this to me as He enters my bitter heart. Lust is not solved through my efforts to 'not be lustful.' Lust *was* forgiven on the cross and Christ reveals this to me as He enters my lustful heart. My hate-filled, jealous, lying, rebellious, resistant old nature is not overcome by working to be something other than what I am. It is annihilated through my death in Christ, not my exertion. The entire work was done on the cross.

Your old sin-loving nature was buried with Him by baptism when He died; and when God the Father, with glorious power, brought Him back to life again, you were given His wonderful new life to enjoy. For you have become a part of Him, and so you died with Him, so to speak, when He died; and now you share His new life and shall rise as He did. Your old evil desires were nailed to the cross with Him; that part of you that loves to sin was crushed and fatally wounded, so that your sin-loving body is no longer under sin's control, no longer needs to be a slave to sin; for when you are deadened to sin you are freed from all its allure and its power over you.

Romans 6:4-7 LB

Living dead is living in Christ. This death is my only Solution. The Father has proven this to humanity throughout the ages. We cannot repair our fallen-ness. But the Good News is, I do not have to repair what He has solved by the Cross. I died with Him, the old sinful man. This is not theoretical or in the future. It is now. All my sin is forgiven and carried away on the cross of Christ. My old nature died with HIM. That nature is no more, it's buried and lost forever.

For the Son of Man came to seek and to save the lost (Luke 19:10). *He has not come to call the righteous but sinners to repentance* (Luke 5:32). *No one can come to Him unless the Father who sent Me draws him. And He will raise him up on the last day* (John 6:44). *All that the Father gives Jesus will come to Him, and whoever comes to Him He will never cast out* (John 6:37).

If Christ is in you, though the body is dead because of sin, yet the spirit is alive because of righteousness (Romans 8:10). *My old self has been crucified with Christ. It is no longer I who live, but Christ lives in me. So, I live in this earthly body by trusting in the Son of God, who loved me and gave Himself for me* (Galatians 2:20). *I am ready for anything through the strength of the One who lives within me* (Philippians 4:13). *For living to me means simply "Christ", and if I die I should merely gain more of Him* (Philippians 1:21). *For in Him we live and move and have our being* (Acts 17:28a).

The Monster Within

As you move forward into living dead, your new creation will come alive in Christ. As individual members of the Body of Christ, we are to be *dead* to our old nature and *alive* in the New. This IS the Body of Christ. The problem is that we actually can live a life separate from Jesus as Source. But living apart from Christ's Life makes us *dismembered* parts of the Body. By functioning on our own, separated from the Head, we are performing either in the dead-self severed from His Body – or worse, claiming to be united while functioning independently and quite apart from Christ our Head.

We, in our new nature, display the living
Christ to a dying world–
not by law and doctrine…but in grace, Spirit, and Truth.

The true Body of Christ is those who have left their will in the grave and now function by the will of Another. Our movements and choices are dictated by Another's mind. His Life is now the source of our life. This is not a doctrinal reaching but a living reality. Outside of His Life, we will only evidence our old dead self, the one from whom we were saved.

The nature of fallen humanity is to consume – to devour in a chewing, munching, eating frenzy. Self is always FOR self with the goal of saving self. Each and every action feeds the existence of self. All is expendable for the will of self's existence. All is subject to the gorging. "What's yours is mine and I will only share what is mine in order to get more of yours!"

Any time you or I do not yield to Christ the Head, regardless of how noble our deeds appear, we function in madness. By nature, we cannot do otherwise. Death seeks life in order to consume it!

Only truly born-again believers have a nature counter to this horrific mode of being. Their existence springs from the fullness of Another.

By grace, I have the very life of the Son of God. And only when I have that precious Life brought forth from my body as my only life, will I have any real life at all.

Think of the horror of the living dead. Monstrous visual, the things of nightmares. But you know, this terror is perpetrated in real life. What is more, it is in the church. It is Christians letting their old nature live while calling it Christ! This is the most frightening horror because the result is actual death and hell.

Jesus solved this terrifying dilemma by CHRIST'S LIFE dwelling in us as our only reality: His mind as my mind, my will surrendered to His will, His LIFE as my life.

Christ's Life is not acquired as a possession to hold, because He is the One holding us. This Life is obtained through receiving Him by faith.

Jesus knows our voracious nature; He created it. But only as He lives through us will we find safety and the hope of satisfaction. When we consent to His indwelling, we receive and experience the Life of the Creator lived through us. It is amazing to observe His Life in my own body, seeing firsthand all that He will do through a life that is simply open to receiving Him.

"My old self has been crucified with Christ. It is no longer I who live, but Christ lives in me. So I live in this earthly body by trusting in the Son of God, who loved me and gave Himself for me."
Galatians 2:20 NLT

You're No Superman

What powers our voracious fallen nature? Ambition! And our culture today fosters ambition – fleshly ambition, spiritual ambition, and soulish ambition. "**Be all you can be and try to appear as more than you actually are!**" Unfortunately, this is a tremendous disservice to those looking for direction. What's more, it cultivates ingratitude and bitterness with God.

There's a problem with a culture where *everyone* gets a trophy, and most are encouraged to be the greatest "ME" possible. This pursuit inevitably fails to relegate that *greater self* to the Will of God. Countless people are sent out thinking they are going to be THE STAR of the Kingdom.

- "You will speak in front of millions and the masses will be saved!"
- "You will prophesy to kings and princes, leaving them speechless!"
- "Your healing ministry will touch hundreds of thousands!"

This is all great if it is true, but for MOST it is not. There are very few Billy Grahams in this world. Am I trying to discourage vision and hope? No, I am contending for the Will of God, which is Christ's Life as my life. If you want to know the will of God, seek the Life of Christ.

If I were called to be the prominent face of a worldwide ministry, then this would be His specific will for me. I would have the grace and His Life to do it. But I am speaking about the masses looking to "go BIG" when they are relegated to something smaller. Anything beyond the Will of God is an ambition that leads to jealousy, coveting, and demonic activity.

Looking at my life, I see that I've never been the figurehead of greatness. All my personal successes have come with minimal exposure. Most have been for God alone. And in this, I have come to a place of peace and desire to defend the Will of God for my life. I do not want more than His will allows!

The Life of Christ in me is a support of another's ministry. I have had the privilege of walking in life and working with Martha Kilpatrick and Shulamite Ministries for over twenty five years now. I'm not the face of Shulamite Ministries; but His Life in me is an integral support of Martha's ministry. This has been a life altering opportunity.

In the early 80's Martha regularly read and listened to Major Ian Thomas from Torchbearers International. Major Thomas' message of the exchanged life captivated her. After one of his meeting at her church she had a conversation with him. I have always loved this dialog!

She first said to him, "I got it!" (meaning the revelation of the exchanged life.) Ian giggled, "You got HIM!" Martha proceeded "How do you live it out?!" Ian responded, "One moment at a time." While this conversation seems simplistic, within this dialog both the quandary and solution is revealed. He is the exchanged life, and it is lived one step at a time.

I believe there was an impartation of Christ's life into Martha and from that His teaming life pours forth. This powerful message—even now—resonates out through her teaching both audio and written. And it has been my privilege to assist her to get her messages out in front of as many people as possible.

Though I have had men come and say, "It is okay, God will advance you soon," I do not look for it or even want that. I want to be in the Will of God for my life, not on the fast track of spiritual advancement. Being relegated to the Will of God is *going big*, the biggest possible.

When we find ourselves scratching and clawing for greatness, we are actually just the world calling ourselves *church*. The Will of God is the only measure of true success and greatness. And to the chagrin of many, His Will does not often mean *public* greatness.

The Will of God is our highest standard of living and the greatest expression of Life we can know. There is no greater life than the one Jesus Christ lives in me. And within His Will is also my complete fulfillment. The Will of God equals Life and His greatness in me!

So do not lose your bold, courageous faith, for you are destined for a great reward! You need the strength of endurance to reveal the poetry of God's will and then you receive the promise in full.
Hebrews 10:35-36 TPT

Apart from Him I Can Do NOthing

As the Director of Shulamite Ministries, I have discovered that there is no end to what Jesus will do when I receive His Life as my own. He made me an audio editor decades ago, and since then, I have recorded and edited hundreds and hundreds of Martha's messages—Shulamite Podcasts, Messages of the Month, and audio series. I say this only to show how very qualified I have become to edit audio files. I am a bit of an audiophile and really strive for excellence. And I tell you this with one purpose in mind: ALL MY EXPERIENCE IS WORTH **ZERO!**

I had a bit of a fiasco while editing some messages Martha delivered at a conference in New Mexico. I jumped into the task and fittingly, the subject of the message was on Christ living our lives. *I* made it through the edit pretty well. All I needed to do was merge the two files I was working on and then save the project. The merge proceeded to the very end and then froze. Guess what happened next? Yeah, you guessed it, the program crashed and my hours of work were GONE! All I had done vanished with one little computer hiccup.

I would love to say I immediately thanked the Lord and sang a hymn, but nope. I screamed. And you know that still small Voice that is oh so convincing and convicting? Well, I heard it over the din of my own screaming. *"You did not give it to Me to do."*

The word of God very, very specifically says, **"But apart from ME you can do nothing."** John 15:5 was the very first scripture I ever memorized as a new believer. You think that was a coincidence? Let's look at this scripture through the lens of this event. "I am the Vine, John, you are just a branch. When you abide in Me and I in you, then your editing will bear much fruit, but apart from Me, your computer is going to crash and eat your work—because on your own, you can do nothing of any value." Actually, it is even more dire than that. I have seen that all my works done in the flesh just whirls up hell. It is not benign; it is *very* malignant.

If it was just me (in the flesh) doing this editing, then the mark of my flesh would stain the recordings going out. People were listening to hear about how Christ lives our lives edited by a man who was not allowing His Life to be mine. In this light, yes, I can thank God for destroying my hours of self-supported rebellion.

It does not matter if I *know* how to do something; the Life of the Son must be the Source of all my doing. I am to be only the observer of His Life flow. What Jesus does is eternal. So, Christ's performance of my life makes my life eternal.

I am the vine; you are the branches.
Whoever abides in Me and I in him, he it is that bears much fruit,
for apart from Me you can do nothing.
John 15:5 ESV

Choosing His Life Over Mine

After I told a friend about this computer crash situation, she asked me, "If the computer had not crashed, would you have seen the task of editing the messages as a success or failure?" This is an *excellent* question! She continued, "This is where I get hung up: not recognizing that my 'success' is failure, too, apart from Jesus."

This is precisely my point and only the Spirit of the Living God can reveal this to us. His job is to lead me into the TRUTH of living in the power of Christ's Life, and then to bring about the reality of His Life, not mine. For though there is a once-and-for-all choice to have Christ live my life, that is not where my choosing ends. Every moment from that original choice will present additional decisions—Jesus or me.

Though the performance of your life is by His Life, walking it out is in each of *your* moments. This is the relationship of choosing. Your fellowship with Christ is walked out moment by moment. This Life is relational, but at any point I can choose to live it out in my own strength.

I cannot tell you how many times "getting the job done" has been my motivation rather than allowing Him to perform my tasks. Even if He is calling me to do something, He still asks to perform the task. And to be perfectly honest, performing the will of God in my flesh sometimes seems easier and more expedient. "It is done, God, there You go!" But the results are often a complete mop-up job and my utter humiliation.

As frightening as this is to consider, Jesus will let you go the hard way and do it yourself. If I decide to live in my own strength, then I can. And as I have heard Martha quote an Episcopal priest many times over the years, "God will let you go to hell if that is absolutely what you want to do." My performance *is* hell!

The crucial choice is whether I want my life to be eternal or merely temporal. Do I want to live my life like a hamster in a spinning wheel or in Christ? My hamster-life is deceptive and misleading. When I perform even my best of intentions, I deceive all around me that it can be done. I wish it was not this black and white, but it is.

The Holy Spirit is the litmus test of this life. He knows and can reveal when Christ's performance is being worked out in our lives. And ultimately, at the end of this life, we will know who it was who lived our lives. Will we hear "Well done, good and faithful servant" or "Depart from me, I never knew you"? The deciding factor is *who was the source* of my doing, and not what I did.

It is about the relationship. His Life as my life is relational, like a dance where He leads. In it you can experience His strength, feel His passions, and know Him as He would reveal Himself to and through you. You cannot be faithful in this, so He will be your faithfulness. He will actually perform where you are unable.

> *The mystery which hath been hid from ages, but now is made manifest to His saints: to whom God would make known what is the riches of the glory of this mystery ...which is Christ in you, the hope of glory.*
> Colossians 1:26-27

I'm Just Like Every Other Tom, Dick, and Harry

It is not always easy to let Jesus be free in you. In my observation, humans by nature love to define and confine other humans. "Just be like me!" It makes us feel safe when those around us are like us. "If your sheep coat smells like my sheep coat, then I must be OK." Yet when we do this, we stymie individuality and the flow of the Spirit and Life of Christ. The fact is, we are not safe in our sameness; our only safety rests in being in the Will of God and Spirit led.

It is just common. We like what we are familiar with, even if that is dysfunctional. Being creatures of habit, change and newness tend to scare us. The true experience of life, however, is found in dependence on God and allowing Him to define your person. Your Creator knows your design better than any other – or even you. I am not promoting being a maverick; I am contending for His Life.

As we walk this globe, we have to fight *for* our God-given design. We have to fight because, unfortunately, every Tom, Dick, and Harry will attempt to clothe us with their ideas of who we should be. They will kindly attempt to convince us that their way is the *best way*. And if it is not others attempting to mold us, then it is us sculpting ourselves. Something will always be pushing against God's blueprint of us.

We must remain committed to God's design for our person. Though it is yours to *discover*, it is not yours to *define*. How Christ wishes to express Himself through your life is the reality that will lead you into His glory. Just imagine, I experience glory when I'm witnessing Christ *in me*. The Bible says, "Christ in me is the hope of glory" (Colossians 1:27). We get the privilege of witnessing His very life in the situations of our lives. There's nothing more practical in your Christian life than to see Him resolve issues and express Himself in your life, through your body. I contend that this is

THE adventure of life. And this is why settling for anything less is a travesty.

Why would I rob myself of seeing Christ's own Life? Why would I allow others or even myself to limit my seeing of Him? Momentary comfort? Fleeting approval? Unity? If all of these are not found within the Life of Christ, then they are merely momentary counterfeits. Only Christ's Life is glory!

We have all experienced the push to conform – those "be like me" moments. Whether that conformity is called for from our families, or in our friendships, by our associations, or even from within ourselves in the deep recesses of our subconscious minds. Very few people will ever support ***Christ in you***. But Christ's Life as my life is the only life that will satisfy. This satisfaction isn't only eternal, it is also practical and tangible in daily reality. Christ in me isn't only my *hope of glory*; He is my only hope to experience the truest adventure of life.

Christ's life was vilified, scandalized, and feared by most. And though the masses flocked to His miracles, how many wanted to snuggle up to the unpredictable nature of His person? Even Jesus' closest followers were puzzled and dismayed by how the Father expressed Himself through His Son. And this will be our experience, too. If we allow Christ's Life to be our life, our lives will be a magnet for the full spectrum of the responses He received.

Christ's Life will be the crushing of every willful, rebellious, self-saving bone in our bodies. But the reward of letting Jesus live our very lives is to see Him and to experience His heart. Living "His Life as my life" is our ringside seats to experiencing His eternal glory, NOW!

And my present life is not that of the old "I", but the living Christ within me. The bodily life I now live, I live believing in the Son of God, who loved me and sacrificed Himself for me.
Galatians 2:20 PHILLIPS

Preventing Christ's Shine

Ye are the light of the world. A city that is set on an hill cannot be hid.

Neither do men light a candle, and put it under a bushel, but on a candlestick; and it giveth light unto all that are in the house.

Let your light so shine before men, that they may see your good works, and glorify your Father which is in heaven.
Matthew 5:14-16 KJV

I saw something while reading this scripture. It is about so much more than simply concealing one's talents or knowledge of the Gospel. I believe it is about restricting the very Life of Christ, who is the Light.

I said in an episode of the Shulamite Podcast, "I wonder if the bushel is not just a cap on what we will accept of Christ's Life and Light. The bushel is literally a cap, a limitation, that I place over His Light coming from out of me." When we prevent Christ's Light-Life from being all that He would want to be in us, we are hiding HIS Light under OUR bushel.

When we prevent Christ the full right of access to our lives, then we cover Light that wants to shine. Now why in the world would we do this? What reason could there be to possibly prevent Light's shine? One reason could be our concepts, labels and opinions of self. "I do not deserve… I'm not ready… I am not worthy…" Foolishness I know, but boy, have I done it.

All our bellybutton gazing really does not help our cause. We surface from the depths with only self-imposed labels and self-consumed attitudes that usually falsely estimate our worth, value, and true condition.

The Spirit of the Living God is the only being that can correctly surmise our true heart condition. Sure, passersby can judge or brand us with a mark, but only the Spirit, however He wishes to come, can truly define us. This is the job of the Spirit.

And when He comes, He will convict and convince the world and bring demonstration to it about sin and about righteousness (uprightness of heart and right standing with God) and about judgment:
John 16:8 AMPC

He tells me where I am, who I am, and where I am not. It is the Spirit's position to lead me into all truth, including about myself.

Where I have wrongly walked in the past is in allowing my opinions of myself to limit Christ's ability to shine forth and glorify His Father. I have placed the lid on the LIFE of Christ in me, because I was looking at *me* rather than Jesus. Where this gets into serious sin is when I limit, prevent, and STOP His shine because I do not think I am worthy!

God help us! Our boxes, labels, and opinions about ourselves are restrictions on Christ. We have the ability to diminish the flow of His Life from within us. All we have to do is cap it beneath the dark cloak of our opinion of self. Or we can 'replace' the true Christ by a fake persona that puts us in the center.

The choice on the table is whether we will abandon our list of labels, throw off our constraining opinions, and let Him Father us, define us, and Shine as He wills through us…or not.

You scrutinize my path and my lying down,
And are intimately acquainted with all my ways.
Even before there is a word on my tongue,
Behold, O Lord, You know it all.
You have enclosed me behind and before,
And laid Your hand upon me.
Psalm 139:3-5 NASB

The Hinderance to Intimate Fellowship

Your old self is a hindrance to your *intimate* fellowship with God. So how do you go about slaying this ungodly hydra robbing you of intimate relationship with Jesus? The simple answer is: the hydra (old self) *is* dead!

I ***have been*** *crucified with Christ. It is no longer I who live, but Christ who lives in me. And the life I now live in the flesh I live by faith in the Son of God, who loved me and gave Himself for me.*
Galatians 2:20 ESV

This old nature died with Christ on the Cross, but this does not preclude our having to go to our own cross of choosing His Life over ours daily. At any point, we can dance with that old nature. Remember our example of the living dead, where Christians let their old nature live while calling it Christ? This is a monstrous dragon.

The fallen nature in unbelievers is an expected evil but the old nature is the true monster. I expect the unsaved to be wretched because they are unregenerate, but the phrase *old nature* communicates that it is something that has passed. My old man is dead but I have to know he is oh-so-willing to rise up from his grave and party. To still be choosing it while appearing as Christ, that is spooky!

God does not have intimate relationship with our old man. This does not mean that He does not speak to him, because God talks to everyone—the serpent, the donkey, Cain, etc. God speaks! But I am talking about an intimate, relational conversation. And more than that, getting to know the One behind the Voice. You do not speak with your spouse as you would a store clerk, and Jesus does not speak to just anyone as He speaks to His Bride.

A new self is required to have intimate relationship with God. The Father has relationship with His Son, and if you want that to include you, then you need His Life in you *as you.*

"...it is no longer I who live, but Christ lives in me..."
Galatians 2:20 NASB

"...this mystery, which is Christ in you, the hope of glory."
Colossians 1:27 HCSB

Fellowship with God is for the Son towards the Father. My life is *in* Him, so there, too, is my fellowship with God. This all is such a spiritual seeing. It took me time to comprehend this truth and I am convinced no words can communicate it sufficiently. This is a revelation I had to have birthed in me through the Spirit.

For you died, and your life is now hidden with Christ in God.
Colossians 3:3 NIV

Here is Oswald Chambers on the matter: *"Is your life truly 'hid with Christ in God'? If it is, your continual request is—'Cause me to hear Thy voice.' Can we hear the voice in which there is no self-realization, no self-interest, no individual preference? Spiritual muddle comes because we have other interests and loyalties, and these loyalties break our intimacy with Jesus Christ. When there is the clash of self-realization, and individual preferences come in and compete, we have to put them on one side and remain loyal to our Lord and to nothing and no one else."*[2]

The old nature is fallen. It is focused on self-awareness and self-interests. The new man is Christ in me. Your current life is hidden in Christ, though you are here. This is a great mystery, the mystery of the Gospel. I know it by revelation and then experience it by faith.

Jesus? Are You in Here?

We either meet Christ in others or we meet their hydra monster. Mankind at its absolute best is wretched. It is monstrous and bestial. I've gone through this world expecting that I, in and of my own self, would be kind, gentle, good and godly. I have failed miserably! I have also looked to others to evidence these traits and found at the core of every human kindness is a fanged foe. In this power of the flesh, I have both soothed like a snake charmer and been hypnotized by the same—it is all so demoniacal. Charm is deceitful and beauty is vain! I ask myself, "Can you not stop your tyrannical expectations and strangling hopes that flesh would display Christ?" Nope. Guess Christ will have to do that, too!

For so long I have looked for others to DO right without having the life of Christ. I grit my teeth in anger thinking, "How can they do that?!" It is very easy to do, without Jesus. And even having the indwelling life of Christ, I can buckle under the legalistic expectations I have of *myself*. "John, why can't you just do that? It is so very simple!" Plainly stated, **the fleshly old nature will never be Christ**.

I have been tested on this. How can I expect the unregenerate to respond with His heavenly Life? I assure you, I can and have! But this course of action has proved to be debilitating and devastating to my spirit. **Christ is the only one who can BE Christ.**

I had a beloved spiritual grandmother in Florida who used to say, "John, we do not even know if the pastor is saved!" Her words always curbed my frustrated expectations. I would think, "**To expect Christ from those who do not have Christ is foolish!**"

I wish this were just in the world, but this is everywhere, even in the church. Just because someone goes to church, or names the name of Jesus, does not necessarily mean they have surrendered to His Lordship and exhibits the Union-Life. I always remember the disciples' question in Matthew 19, "Who then can be saved?" This rings so true when one is passing through this earth.

What is the answer to this dilemma? "Let Christ" and stop expecting Him to appear where He has not been made Lord. Be His sheep and live under Him as Shepherd. If I stopped laying expectations on others, and myself, maybe Christ's Life in me would recognize Christ in others and I would not be so affected by where He is not.

Maybe instead of being offended, I would pray for His life to invade.
Maybe I would stop playing Holy Spirit and *let Him do His work.*
Maybe I would see the miraculous if I stopped focusing on the maniacal.

At the end of every day, He is GOD and I am NOT. **Christ is the only one who can BE Christ in this world!**

> *With eyes wide open to the mercies of God, I beg you, my brothers, as an act of intelligent worship, to give Him your bodies, as a living sacrifice, consecrated to Him and acceptable by Him. Do not let the world around you squeeze you into its own mould, but let God re-mould your minds from within, so that you may prove in practice that the plan of God for you is good, meets all His demands and moves towards the goal of true maturity.*
> Romans 12:1-2 PHILLIPS

Talking About the Music or Played as an Instrument

Some people talk about the music while others are played as an instrument. I have met many people who discuss the beauty of Christ. They speak about the beauty of His music and their enjoyment of His sound. But what they are missing is being played as His instrument. Yes, being played as His instrument to make music. He does not just desire us to talk about His Life; He yearns for us to experience Him as He breathes His Life through us.

This is the mystery of the Gospel and the secret to life. That's right, I defined *the secret to life!* This is what the Apostle Paul preached in his letters and what has been hidden throughout the ages but is now being revealed in the end times. This *is* the mystery of the Gospel! **No longer should we merely talk about the music, now we can be *played* as His instrument.**

I've heard Martha describe this as the glory of the New Covenant. Christ in you is our hope of glory and this is the New Covenant. The New Covenant is this: **Christ does it *all*.** And I can talk about this endlessly, or I can choose to be played as His instrument. It is my choice. But the fact remains: speaking about it does not make it so.

This is an experiential reality alone. And in that experience, you experience Christ, see Christ, and know Christ up close and personally in your own body. He becomes your life and fulfills His own requirements of the Law. This is the New Covenant.

Hallelujah, your endless struggle to *be* godly is over in His fulfillment of His requirement! You are but an instrument for Him to play His life through, and while being played, you learn who He is. He did not just give us a theoretical example of His Life – He is your life. Right here, right now, you get to see how He would respond in your life situations. This is so beyond just hearing how it would work; *it is seeing how it* ***does*** *work.*

The Boy Who Just Talked About It

This reminds me of a story I heard about a little boy who visited the North Georgia mountains. A day had been planned where all the children would go tubing and then have lunch. Everyone got loaded up and proceeded to the river. When they arrived, all that could be seen and heard was squeals of joy and arms flailing. This was going to be so much fun. All but one child got into the river and began to float and splash. A lone, little boy chose to stay on the riverbank and walk along as the others floated next to him. He watched, he giggled, and seemingly enjoyed his time. Later at lunch, as the event was discussed, this little boy described the event as if he had participated as well. You would have thought he was leading them all down the river. In his mind, he was in the river though he never even got wet.

This is how many Christians live today. They *talk* about the Life of Christ while failing to ever get in the river. This is tragic because everything has been provided for our adventure. We are to *experience* the Gospel as He lives it through us.

Now unto Him that is able to do exceeding abundantly above all that we ask or think, according to the power that worketh in us, Unto Him [be] glory in the church by Christ Jesus throughout all ages, world without end. Amen.

Ephesians 3:20-21 ASB

Hasta La Vista, Self!

Who will deliver me from this body of death?
Romans 7:24 ESV

I am imprisoned in a body of death. I am set as a slave to serve and focus on it. I'm mindful of its complaints, its aches, and its inconveniences. It plagues me day and night: if it is not this, it is that. This body wants, desires, demands and expects. My involvement is continual and staggeringly consistent. I wait on it hand and foot. I serve it as one would a petulant king. With but a single thought, I notice and succumb to the demands. I bow when it whines and yield when it calls. In sickness, I am searching to make it well; in hunger, I passionately seek to satisfy the urge.

I am the endless servant of SELF!

I am cold, I am hot, I'm hungry, I'm tired, I need Tums®, I have a headache, fetch me a pillow, bring me a beer, I've got to use the restroom, I do not like sitting this way, that breeze is too strong, that sun is too bright, I cannot think over that noise, itch my back, adjust my shoe, brush that hair from my face, my nails are too long, I need to go walk and clear out my head, this is too strenuous, take me back home, my eyes feel dry, my pants are too tight, I feel nauseated, roll over I'm not comfortable, I'm thirsty, turn on the light I cannot see, ooh what is that substance dripping out of my nose . . . on and on the drone of noise issues out from this walled prison. Despot of despots, one we cannot escape.

How else is this body of death affected? The environment and things that I ingest are killing me slowly by degrees. Things that I must have to survive, poison me in this prison of skin. Acid rain, GMOs, pesticides on my food, smog in my air, chemicals in my water, carcinogens in containers that hold my food, toxins injected into or added to my food to make it bigger, last longer, or look fresher. Dead from within and death coming from without.

Please Lord, deliver me from this **BODY OF DEATH**!

Solution? **Christ!** He is your health. He is your own endurance to your own prison. He is your satisfaction. He is the only one who can accept and receive His very own order. Jesus made you, made this world, made the order of all things, and He will have to be everything in you to receive, accept, and embrace it all. The answer to all our woes is *HE Himself* being our life. We cannot shut our body up from its demands. We cannot stop eating pollutants, and even if we could…it wouldn't help. God Himself bound you to a body of death for the purpose of annihilating your independence of HIM. You are not supposed to fix it, adjust it, or change it. No, you are supposed to say yes to His order and surrender to Him who can do it all. He is the only one who does not rage against the machine. He is the only one who doesn't curse God in frustration for the fall of all of creation. It isn't what the Lord can do or has done—it is JESUS! He is your only Solution.

The Bondage of Remaining the Same

Anywhere that I am in the flesh, I am a slave. There is only One Life that is not the slave-life and that is the Life of Christ. Every other attempt to live this life is from *self* and slavery. Yes, our every attempt is slavery. Our life apart from Christ's Life is slavery. So, if we are working, living, being in the flesh, then we are slaves. ONE Life and only One Life is free from slavery—Christ's.

I expect this from blatant sin; for if I am in sin, I am a slave to sin. But what of the good that I do, is that included? Yes, if I am doing it then it is slavery. This is because in myself I ***am*** a slave to sin. My old nature is the slave nature. The only solution to this state of being is to die.

Anywhere I am in the flesh, I am in sin. Is this taking it too far? Could this be true? Is everything I do sin, bar Christ's own performance? Yes, I believe so. It is all about source. "*A good tree* ***cannot*** *produce bad fruit, and a bad tree* ***cannot*** *produce good fruit*" (Luke 6:43 NLT). Our nature inherited from Adam and Eve is a sin nature. This nature is a bad tree. By choosing the Tree of Knowledge, we chose the bad tree from which NO good comes. The self-life is sin-life.

Look at Abraham and his children. The difference between the slave and the freewoman and the children they bore was simply this: "*I Do It!*" or "*God Does It!*" From the freewoman has come the child of promise and line of Christ. "*You Samaritans know very little about the One you worship, while we Jews know all about Him,* ***for salvation comes through the Jews***" (John 4:22 NLT). God chose to bring His blessing through the line of Isaac. Whereas Ishmael, the fruit of the slave woman, even to this day, is death and destruction. The effort of Sarah and Abraham to "assist" God has brought about heartache and contention from then on. And with this being said, God's grace is still able to overcome.

The flesh can do nothing but serve self and love self. There is no faith in flesh, and without faith it is impossible to please God (Hebrews 11:6). Flesh only believes in what serves self – this is not faith. If I *can* do or perform it, I need no faith, only belief that I can. On the other hand, Christ's Life always serves the Father and surrenders to His Will. His Life is the Life that we have been given to reign in us. His mysterious Life expresses His Life, Love, and Will in and through you. This is the ONLY Life that pleases the Father, and the only Life that gains eternal reward and expresses His Kingdom reality.

The work to receive this is just a 'yes.' I have believed even the exchanged Life was about my effort. But, no! It is as easy as, "Yes Father, I choose You over me." And with this agreement, His Life begins to express itself through us. There isn't an effort or striving to make it happen, there's only the work to *believe*. To have faith that Christ is your Life and faith that He desires to live His Life through you.

Facing the Curse on Man

Why do men get so aggravated while working with electronics or mechanical things? This was my assistant's question after witnessing my attempts to install a new phone system that was fighting me badly. I laughed and said, "I know exactly why: because it rubs up against our curse."

This has become a point of humor. For instance, in my favorite Christmas movie, *A Christmas Story*, this is perfectly depicted. Mr. Parker, Ralphie's father, wrestled with his furnace, expletives flying. It was an epic battle and a crusade of male human strength – "**I will conquer this**!" The machines always seem to throw a wrench into my life work.

"Cursed is the ground because of you; through painful toil you will eat food from it all the days of your life."
Genesis 3:17 NIV

Men know full well the repercussions of the fall, and it is not relegated to the growing of food. We feel it, experience it, and struggle with it daily. The natural man is tied to the effects of the curse and the painful toil hurts our souls. This is the fall and we hate it! The consequence of sin is always a bitter pill to swallow.

When talking to my assistant, I poised it in a more dramatic light. "We know when the thorns and thistles are tearing at our flesh and we hate it! Isn't it supposed to succumb to my dominion?!" Spoken like a true man.

There is a solution! The New Man is not hindered by the curse. The world is fallen, so I do not know if we can truly live unaffected by the fall. This world is ordered around the fall – "Both thorns and thistles it shall grow for you." But I *do* know that the New Life in the

New Man gives us HIS own ability to have Another's Life face the curse. Christ's Life is not subject to the fall because He is sinless.

In His power and strength, I am not entangled by my labors. This does not mean I do not have to work, it just means the source of my life is His Life, not mine. He can navigate through His world, where I am just frustrated by it.

These things I have spoken to you, that in Me you may have peace. In the world you will have tribulation; but be of good cheer, I have overcome the world."
John 16:33 NKJV

Living Free of Anxiety

The old nature will always fret. From Adam and Eve until today, the old creation will always be in anxiety. You can count on it like clockwork. You may not acknowledge it as anxiety or call it anxiety, but the SELF-LIFE is anxious. It is only the NEW creation in Christ that will dwell in Peace. If we are attempting to conquer anxiety in the flesh, we will fail. Christ's Life, as my life, is *the only life* which remains free of anxiety. I know this chaps some people, because the old nature does not like being that vulnerable to God. Plus the self-life will bargain, beg or steal to do it in self-strength. But victory is only assured if we approach this issue, **as every issue**, in the New Man who is Christ.

Put off your old self, which belongs to your former manner of life and is corrupt through deceitful desires, and to be renewed in the spirit of your minds, and to put on the new self, created after the likeness of God in true righteousness and holiness.
Ephesians 4:22-24 ESV

If you sweep the house clean of your old life, then you can have it filled with HIS Life. Once you put off that old sinful, wicked, independent life, then you can trust in God's Life to be your life. You are but a shell, He is the filling.

This is the only answer to anxiety, stress, hypertension, fear, and trepidation about life. Christ must be your life. Not imitation, not leading, not guidance, no – the indwelling LIFE. Jesus doesn't assist me or point me in the right direction. **He lives my actual life.**

Since you have been raised to new life with Christ, set your sights on the realities of heaven, where Christ sits in the place of honor at God's right hand. Think about the things of heaven, not the things of earth. **For you died to this life, and your real life is hidden with Christ in God**. *And when Christ,* **<u>who is your life</u>**, *is revealed to the whole world, you will share in all His glory.*
Colossians 3:1-4 NLT

The Pivot of Belief

Anxiety is incredible unbelief in God's ability to perform my tasks. Anxiety is unbelief in Christ's very Life to perform His will and purpose in mine. So if anxiety is unbelief, then what is it that we are actively believing *in*? Humans by nature are believers. We will believe in something, even if that something is false. That is just how we were made.

If anxiety is unbelief in God's ability to live our life, then what *are we* believing in? Hardship! Anxiety is faith in difficulty and struggle. It says that life will always be too hard or impossible. It is a false faith. Unfortunately, we will manufacture calamity in our life circumstances to support our anxiety. It is like some "virgin thrown into the volcano" act of worship.

If I am a believer in trouble, hardship, and difficulty, I will bring it about. I will not be wrong. It is crazy, right? Why would I purposely sabotage the course of my life? To support my *god*—anxiety. Yes, if I am in anxiety I am in fear and that is not faith in God, it is the *worship* of fear.

It is like an Eeyore spirit, but not so cute: ever the pessimist about all of life. Not only is it my view, but also it becomes my reality. The frightening thing with this is that even if there is not true calamity, our faith in it makes us blind to reality. We will believe in the difficulty whether it is there or not. This is the power of belief!

Now, I am not shoving ice picks into my tires or lighting my unfiled tax returns on fire just to be anxious. No, it is less obvious than that. The anxious person literally sets things up to be anxious. Have you ever seen someone tackle a major enterprise in the middle of a trying time? Like, "Hey, I am going to remodel my house, while I am preparing for my daughter's wedding!" I have seen it over and over and done it more than I wish to admit. It is believing in the energy and motivation found in anxiety and using it like a tool. The problem is, I END UP BEING THE TOOL! We make subtle choices that bring about deliberate chaos.

God will perfectly lay out our tasks in the Spirit. It is like a road map with landmarks, asking us to invite Him in to perform our lives. Christ's course is His will and choices. But when we take control and pop a wheelie, God help us! Listening to the nudgings of the flesh will make for dire deals.

For it is God who works in you,
both to will and to work for His good pleasure.
Philippians 2:13 NKJV

Life is an invitation for God's participation. We have the unique ability to choose for ourselves whether or not He is given permission to perform our lives. It is all set up for us to yield to His Life.

The false faith of anxiety feeds on tension, while Christ's life is about rest. It is not just an option; it is how to live. When you lay these two paths side by side, it all comes down to one fact: anxiety is rebellion. Either Christ lives my life and I enter His rest, or I give the reins of my life to anxiety and live in torment.

Therefore, while the promise of entering His rest still stands,
let us fear lest any of you should seem to have failed to reach it.
Hebrews 4:1 ESV

The Cross Life Crosses Me Out

Now let's look at the glorious side of being anxious. Yes, there is a positive aspect to this sin. The benefit is its magnification of three things: our utter dependence on Jesus, our need for continual relationship with the Father, and the necessity to increase our knowledge of God. It is there where our personal cross meets Christ in us.

Christ as me does not allow me to bypass *me* in an avoidance of responsibility. I do not simply choose Christ's Life over my life and I am done with it. No, Christ's Life unearths every bit of me, regularly. I have to die to every selfish, sinful bone in my body. His Life paves the way for my repentance and personal crosses. I am not afforded an easy bypass around. Quite the contrary, I am assured of a direct routing to deal with self. Christ's Life is the Light of exposure that beams upon all that is *not* Christ in me. Though choosing Christ's Life over your own is the way of grace and glory, it is not a "get out of jail free" card. You still have to face your life and sinful nature.

Again, there is a once and for all choice, but it does not end there. You give the Father your yes to Christ's Life in exchange for yours, but there's also a daily choosing of His Life in preference to your own. Why? Why would the Father design it this way? Because this life is about dependence upon, relationship with, and an increase in your knowledge of Christ. This life's design is for knowledge and interaction with your God. Regardless of how we may desire our independence from God, this life is intended to foster our union with – *not separation from* – God.

This is such liberty! But even beyond that there is an element that is awe-inspiring—bridal preparation. Christ's Life as my life is our preparation for being the Bride of Christ, as well as cleansing us from all that hinders our being that Bride. Love is volitional. *Loving is a choice.* And with this in mind, the weakness of man just becomes another facilitator to express our love.

Daily choosing Jesus over self is an expression of our love and develops our relationship as Bride and Bridegroom. Knowing that the crosses we face in this life are but Christ's preparation of us, as He lives His Life through us, helps us to embrace rather than wince at them. The cross is always redemptive, not punitive, but without exception, you have the choice of either receiving or resisting it. Though you can avoid your crosses in this life and live for self, you cannot have Christ live His Life in you without facing your crosses. By nature, light dispels darkness, and this will be your experience if you prefer His Light over your darkness.

> *Let us rejoice and shout for joy! Let us give Him glory and honor, for the marriage of the Lamb has come [at last] and His bride (the redeemed) has prepared herself." She has been permitted to dress in fine linen, dazzling white and clean—for the fine linen signifies the righteous acts of the saints [the ethical conduct, personal integrity, moral courage, and godly character of believers].*
>
> Revelation 19:7-8 AMP

Saving My Life, Looses My Life

The Word declares that if I save my life, I will lose my life, but if I lose my life, then I gain Life (see Matthew 10:39, Matthew 16:25, Mark 8:35, Luke 9:24, and John 12:25). I have a new revelation for what this means. **Saving my life is me living my life, rather than letting Christ BE my Life!** If you keep your life, maintain your life, live your life in your own strength and power, then you are trying to save it. To lose your life is to let Christ's Life be your life, which consequentially saves your life.

If you cling to your life, you will lose it; but if you give up your life for Me, you will find it.
Matthew 10:39 NLT

All who seek to live apart from Me will lose it all. But those who let go of their lives for My sake and surrender it all to Me will discover true Life!
Matthew 10:39 TPT

This scripture has been a banner over my life. The Lord confronted me with John 12:25 as a small child: *"He who loves his life will lose it, and he who hates his life in this world will keep it for eternal life."* To love your life is to lose your life. But with my new insight, I understand it more than I ever have. God was always addressing His Life over mine.

I, like everyone, have witnessed the train wreck of being the source of my life. It was like running blindfolded and covered in Crisco straight into the Tea Cup ride at Disney World with my hands full of knives. Someone is going to get stabbed! But Jesus gave us His Life to save our lives. I do not have to right the sinking ship; **I have a Life-Preserver**.

Then Jesus said to His disciples, "If anyone wants to follow in My footsteps he must give up all right to himself, take up his cross and follow Me. For the man who wants to save his life will lose it; but the man who loses his life for My sake will find it. For what good is it for a man to gain the whole world at the price of his own soul? What could a man offer to buy back his soul once he had lost it?
Matthew 16:24-26 PHILLIPS

Bring God Into It!

A life without Christ is aptly described as a sinking ship. And our world is filled with that level of desperation. We do many things to mask and silence the need but still it remains—a gnawing hunger demanding to be satisfied. We cannot escape it; it is the fallen human condition. In the Garden of Eden, we opened a cavern by excavating God from our hearts, and that void requires filling. Yet nothing satisfies our attempts to fill the void, because God is the only satisfaction for that gaping maw of need.

If your eyes are open even a little, you will see the terrible need of humanity all around you. I swim laps several times a week, and one morning as I drove to the pool, I got stuck behind a school bus. The bus stopped at a dilapidated, single-wide trailer. On the stoop stood two little children ready for school and a very unkempt looking mother. She perched there in a dirty bathrobe, smoking a cigarette. When the bus stopped, the children sprinted to it through the fog, and the mother flicked her cigarette off the stoop and shuffled back into her trailer. No kiss goodbye, no wave from the children – it looked like such a bedraggled existence.

Now, I do not know anything about the lives of this family. Any number of things could have been happening here. All I saw was a brief snapshot, but it made my heart hurt. And I said to God, "What do I do with this?" My question was not really about this poor family. It was broader in its scope. "God, what am I to do with this world?" And He replied, "Bring Me into it."

When I grieve at life situations, God says, "Bring Me into it." When things look depressing, God says, "Bring Me into it." If I am the dwelling place of the Most High, then when I see something, He is seeing it through my eyes. When I feel something, He is feeling it through my heart. So if it *is* Christ in me, then I *can* bring Him into the world, and leave it with Him.

Not only can the Life of Christ bear the pain, He is the Solution to it. And we are the vessels carrying His Life into the world that just needs Jesus.

"Let go of your concerns! Then you will know that I am God. I rule the nations. I rule the earth."
Psalm 46:10 GW

The Struggle to Encounter The Great Exchange

**"A dead Christ I must do everything for;
a living Christ does everything for me."**

Andrew Murray
(South African writer, teacher and Christian pastor, 1828-1917)

Grace is not the freedom to sin, but the freedom not to sin. Grace is God's heart extending itself towards us as He initiates in us the ability to overcome our weaknesses, failures, and inadequacies.

Major Ian Thomas
(evangelist, writer, teacher and founder of
Torchbearers Bible schools 1914-2007)

Christ in Me, Is Not ME

Immanuel is "God with us." Our lives, in their totality, are intended to be lived *with* Him. He wants to live in us, through us, and with us during our entire life. Christ came to dwell among us and now He wants to live *in* us. We are to take Him into every situation of our lives as *He lives* and I observe.

Immanuel became God with us in the deepest sense. Deep within! Where Christ came into the world to be with us, upon His death and resurrection He became God *within* us through His Spirit. And at that point He also became God *as* us. Not only did He come to save us, He came to *be* us.

Jesus Christ desires to be in and involved in ALL of your life. You are to take Him into every situation. I once thought that He wished to dwell in just the spiritual circumstances, but now I know it is everything and everywhere.

We do not have to muster the energy to endure our lives and situations; we are to go in with Jesus. You and I face everything, from our greatest besetting sin to our easiest daily errand, *with Him, in Him*. We do not do anything alone, *ever* again—Christ with us, in everything and forever.

Going to get a loaf of bread from the store? Christ with us! Working at a job? Christ with us! Struggling with a sin? Christ with us! I do not have to do anything on my own. Immanuel, "God with us," is Christ in us, *as us*, today and forever.

"Therefore the Lord Himself will give you a sign: Behold, a virgin will be with child and bear a son, and she will call His name Immanuel.
Isaiah 7:14 NASB

"Behold, I am with you and will keep you wherever you go, and will bring you back to this land; for I will not leave you until I have done what I have promised you."
Genesis 28:15 ESV

All this happened to fulfil what the Lord had said through the prophet—Behold, a virgin shall be with child, and bear a son, and they shall call his name Immanuel. ("Immanuel" means "God with us.")
Matthew 1:23 PHILLIPS

I am with you all the days (perpetually, uniformly and on every occasion) to the [very] close and consummation of the age.
Matthew 28:20b AMPC

Possessing a New Me

There is a secret to Christ with us and union with God and it does not stroke our ego or fleshly pride. It is not about something we perform well or a standard we attain. I would have loved it to be a series of to-do's that I could perform. This way I could protect my heart in case I failed to reach my goal. But no, this secret to union with God exposes me to the whole gamut of emotion.

To enter this place of intimacy with God, I need to possess a new life. My old self was not cutting the mustard because it was not truly interacting with God as I would have liked. I am not primarily speaking of salvation here. I was saved but I was not accessing *all* that His atonement obtained for me. At salvation we are made new. The problem is that we often do not see it or live in that newness.

Do not lie to one another, seeing that you have put off the old self with its practices and have put on the new self, which is being renewed in knowledge after the image of its Creator.
Colossians 3:9-10 ESV

The Amplified Bible quotes verse 10 like this: *And have clothed yourselves with the new [spiritual self], which is [**ever in the process of being**] renewed and remolded into [**fuller and more perfect knowledge** upon] knowledge after the image (the likeness) of Him Who created it.*

My new man has new ears and a new heart. This new life is the basis of every deep relational interaction with God. I have been given a new nature. Actually, I am entirely a New Creation and by faith I receive it. The old me will never be quiet or still. It cannot, and my wrestling with that self is futile; I must let it die.

Therefore, if anyone is in Christ, he is a new creation.
The old has passed away; behold, the new has come.
2 Corinthians 5:17 ESV

The hindrance is only ever me, the *old me* who makes deals with God like an Arab merchant. The one who tries and tries, only to fail. So who is responding to God's invitation to fellowship – the old me or my new creation? WHO is my source?

What Christ in Me Looks Like

I have an amazing picture of the reality of Galatians 2:20: *I have been crucified with Christ and I no longer live, but Christ lives in me. The life I now live in the body, I live by faith in the Son of God, who loved me and gave Himself for me.* I think the Spirit gave me this example as an object lesson of this scripture. It is pictured in the books of the Gospels. While each of these books are the inerrant Living Word of God, they nonetheless maintain the individual expression and personality of the writer. The Gospels came through men, and the voice of each is as different as the men themselves.

This is a paradox extraordinaire, but it is also a major clue into how our lives can be "Christ's life as my life is **His** life in *my* life, and that's not my life as His life, it is HIM." This revelation is illuminating and empowering!

Judging myself and criticizing who I am or am not is debilitating. Labeling myself and then confessing that label is utterly destructive. "I am so stupid! I can never do anything right! I am ugly! I am such a failure!" Whether I formulate these judgments from the opinions of others or it is my own disapproval for my failings, these opinions capture my life and prevent me from being **who I am in Christ**. Placing faith in opinion, whether my own or that of another, circumvents my *actual* reality—who Christ says I am.

Christ designed me with a personhood, which He has matched in His plan and purpose for my life. When I hold myself to old opinions or labels, I derail the reality of the true me. I am who Christ says I am and my life is His Life. Like the example of the Gospels, I am not lost in His expressed Life through me. It is *me*, while still being *Him*.

The *Book of John* is all God, expressed totally through John. John, the person, is visible in his writings, while God's revelation is likewise not obscured. This is the way it is in my life. Christ's Life can be His living expression, while still being me. Now I am not saying that my life is infallible like the Gospels, but I am saying my life can be *all* Him. I have the choice, but leaving my opinions of myself is a must.

Here is another simple visual to express the reality of the indwelling Life of Christ as seen through us. When making cookies with a cookie press, the shape of the form comes through a tip. This makes different shapes, from ribbons, to stars, to dollops, but the dough and substance of the cookie is the same. The shape is expressed through the individuality of the tip, but the substance of the delicious cookies is the dough. In the same way, God is the source of our life, and it is His choice to bring His Life through us. I can at any point choose to believe my opinions over His idea of me, but that is *not* the victorious Life.

Do I Lose Myself?

Do I lose me when Christ *is* me? Is my person eliminated in this transaction? Do I cease to exist because *He* now is my life? If you have never had these thoughts, indulge me for a moment. My friend Bruce commented on this issue, and I think the point he made is vital.

> "You say, 'Not only did Jesus come to save us, He came to be us.' I know what you mean by this, and I agree! However, just for clarification… Jesus never lost His identity in the context of His Father. Even at the end He said, 'Not MY will, but YOUR will…'"

Remember in the last section I told you the banner over my life: *"He who has found his life will lose it, and he who has lost his life for My sake will find it"* (Matthew 10:39). I'll go into this in a few chapters but when I was but a three-and-a-half-year-old child, God was telling me that this was the choice I would have to make throughout my life.

Now that I am over 50 years old, I can look back and see everywhere the Lord was presenting that choice to me. It was not like it was a threat or an ultimatum. It was His excited invitation. "Your life lived is a loss, but My Life found as your life is true Life." It was not a punishment, as if I were losing something valuable. Quite the contrary, I was being liberated from a weight of slavery to live in His glorious Life. **"Lose what has made you lost and find that which will save you."** My lost-life is a loss of every hindrance, and my found-Life is the gaining of God Himself.

His call of me from the beginning (and I would say this is for all of us) was to exchange my life—mine for His. His desire was to give me the best, by delivering me from the worst. Again, it is not punishment or abuse to lose what is killing you; rather it is the call to enter God's eternal, everlasting glory.

So I ask again, do I lose me when Christ *is* me? Did I lose my personality with this loss of life? Absolutely! Did I lose my personhood? Absolutely not! There's a big difference between my personality and my personhood. A personality changes according to source of life. If I live for myself and in my personality, whether good or bad, it is devilish. But if I live in Jesus, my life is spiritual, a journey of knowing and experiencing Him. Personalities are fickle and can evolve and manifest based on circumstances and situations. My unique, individual personhood, however, is God-given. Personhood is God's dream of me.

My Life and personhood are for ONE thing: my yes to Christ. This is the intended purpose. My expression of living is to say yes to His Life. How His Life will express itself through me is unique and individual, but the source of the life is intended to be Christ. My individuality is not lost, it is expressed and uniquely manifested as He chooses to live.

So, did Christ unplug me when He came to be me? Am I no longer present in me because now it is *only* Christ? No. Christ in me is *we.* We are in union. We are one. I am born-again into a New Creature who is Him and me. This is the paradox. I am both in the heavens and in my body with Him. *It is a mystery.* The mystery of the Gospel is Christ in me, my hope of glory. It is not cut and dry and linear; it is more circular. The complete reality is so beyond reason and understanding—it is THE mystery!

By Grace Alone

Paul said it was *by grace alone* that God chose to reveal His Son **in him**. By grace! His revealing is not from our desire, as earnest as it may be, nor through our efforts to have it be so. It is simply God's grace—His unmerited favor. It is His choice and His desire to reveal Christ in me. Though we can ask for it, Jesus' Life is still only expressed by His grace and choosing.

But even before I was born, God chose me and called me by His marvelous grace. Then it pleased Him to reveal His Son to me so that I would proclaim the Good News about Jesus to the Gentiles. When this happened, I did not rush out to consult with any human being.
Galatians 1:15-16 NLT

Christ's revealing of His Life in me is for His pleasure and purpose, not mine. Living in a world infused with self-focus and self-fulfillment, that statement seems almost profane. *"Not about ME?! Who knew!"* Nope. I am a beneficiary, I am blessed, I am satisfied, but the focus is not *for me,* it is for Him.

Look at the scripture again. Paul received the exchanged life *"so that"* God could proclaim the Gospel to the Gentiles. It was not to fulfill Paul's deep heart *for* fellowship and union with God. It was not to satisfy Paul's need *for* a purpose-driven life. And it was not even *for* the people to whom Paul was called. It was for God's satisfaction, for His pleasure and by His plan. This world is for Him, not me!

Does this mean that Paul was not given deep fellowship and union with God, a purpose for his life, or a service to the people of his calling? Certainly not. The reality though is that it was not sourced in Paul's life or under Paul's direction. Paul's fulfillment came from

Christ's own satisfaction. It was the grace of God to reveal His Son's Life in Paul, and *in that grace* was Paul's pleasure.

It is No Longer About You

When you truly belong to Jesus, then this life is no longer about you. This is a hard lesson to learn and I need it repeated again and again. *When my life is truly the Lord's, then this life is no longer about me.* What do I mean by this? Well, when Christ's Life is my life, then it is "not I but Christ" who lives. And as a result, people respond to *Christ in me,* not to me. I do not have to take things personally, whether negative or positive, because it is all about Jesus, not me.

This is not true of ***everyone*** who calls themselves a Christian, by the way. This only applies to those living the Exchanged Life seen in Galatians 2:20.

I have been crucified with Christ and I no longer live, but Christ lives in me. The life I now live in the body, I live by faith in the Son of God, who loved me and gave Himself for me.
Galatians 2:20 NIV

A few years ago, a man came to my house to do some work. He was a really nice guy and I enjoyed talking to him off and on throughout the day. Because of some difficulties with his equipment, he had to spend most of the day at my house but he never got aggravated or angry. At one point, he had to leave to go back to his shop and said he might not be back that day. He asked if I was in a rush to get this job done. I said that I was not. He assured me that he would not delay things, but it might be the following week before he could finish.

After he left I thought he was gone for the day, but lo and behold, he came back within the hour. He was going to get it done for me. And the amazing thing was he was in no hurry to leave.

He finished the job, making sure it was exactly how I wanted it, but then stuck around. Not like a pest, more like he was enjoying being at my house and hanging out. I asked God, "Why is this man lingering?" And the Lord answered, "Me!" Jesus in me loved him, and we do not run from love. Actually, we tend to do everything we can to receive it.

I do not believe this man was born-again or even religious, but he responded to love. And Christ's love was not verbally stated nor even overtly expressed through me. I just talked to him and showed concern for the plight of his equipment difficulties. Christ's love communicates itself quite effectively with a willing vessel who gets out of the way.

And that is the challenge: getting out of the way. It is far too easy to take things personally in this world. Whether negative or positive, it does not matter. If my eyes are on me, I will take things personally. Yet if I am in Christ's Life, it is about Him and no longer about me. Sure, I can get in the flesh and make things about me; I have that choice. But if I remain "**in Him**" then my life is hidden in the heavens and His Life is what people see.

Response to His Life comes as persecution or affection. Jesus was the most loved and hated man the world has ever seen; and if my life is His Life, I will receive the full gamut of man's reaction. Making my life about me is just going to muddy the waters. Either I will become defensive like a hateful honey badger or a self-focused hoarder like a lovesick hamster.

This life is not about *me*! Not the love and not the hatred. Christ in me is the focus. Always.

But if Christ is in you, though the body is dead because of sin, ***the Spirit*** *is life because of righteousness.*
Romans 8:10 NRSV

But thanks be to God, who always leads us in triumph ***in Christ****, and manifests* ***through us*** *the sweet aroma of the* ***knowledge of Him*** *in every place. For we are a fragrance of Christ to God among those who are being saved and among those who are perishing; to the one an aroma from death to death, to the other an aroma from life to life. And who is adequate for these things? For we are not like many, peddling the word of God, but as from sincerity, but as from God, we speak in Christ in the sight of God.*
2 Corinthians 2:14-17 NASB

Do You Meet My Need, or Jesus?

In my early life, I walked this earth strutting my need. When we are wounded, we can be a sucking vortex of need rather than our true person. It is like we are looking for someone to fix us, to heal us, to meet our needs. The problem is that most people reject and resist a demand for comfort.

We know when someone wants something from us, and we instinctively know when it is illegitimate. When that happens, we tend to run the other way. But a needy person only feels the rejection, which then feeds their need even more, making them needier. It is a vicious cycle.

So then, when people meet us, do they meet *our neediness* or Jesus? When we walk through the world, is it "Christ" or "me" they see? I assure you, One gives while the other takes, and One is Life and the other death.

But something strange happens when you allow your life to be Christ in you. When people meet Jesus in us, He often elicits from them the very response that addresses our personal need. Is it not odd that when I deny myself and let my needy old man die, then Christ's resurrected Life satisfies those very needs? The very thing we are looking for is found when we remain in Christ.

We are to be a living tabernacle of Christ's Life and presence. We are indwelt by the Living God, which means we carry His presence everywhere we go. But if I travel through this world peddling my needs, I hide His Light beneath my bushel, so to speak. On the other hand, if I allow Christ's Life and Light to shine, not only do I experience Him but I am satisfied in the core of my being. My so-pervasive need withers away in Him. And there is no amount of panhandling which can ever amass the contentment I receive in Jesus.

But thanks be to God, who always puts us on display in Christ and through us spreads the aroma (fragrance) of the knowledge of Him in every place.
2 Corinthians 2:14 HCSB

Attempting to find someone who might meet my needs is an exercise in futility. We were never designed to live like this. We were fashioned to carry the Living Christ in our world and let His Life impact that landscape. While it is not easy to choose to embrace the cross and deny self, it is the most fruitful and eternal choice we make.

Because the God who said, **Out of darkness light shall shine**, *is the One who shined in our hearts to illuminate the knowledge of the glory of God in the face of Jesus Christ. But we have this treasure in earthen vessels that the excellency of the power may be of God and not out of us."*
2 Corinthians 4:6-7 RV

I am an Ark of His Presence

Let's go deeper into that last thought. I am to carry the presence of God into my world just as the Jewish priests in the wilderness carried the Holy Ark of the Covenant into theirs. Yes, I am literally a carrier of the presence of the living God. More precisely stated, I carry ***Him*** everywhere I go. This is the reality of every *true* Christian *in* Christ. We should expect this as a fact. If you are indwelt by Jesus Christ and His Life resides in you, then you are to usher Him into each and every circumstance you encounter.

But thanks be to God, who always puts us on display in Christ and through us spreads the aroma (fragrance) of the knowledge of Him in every place.
2 Corinthians 2:14 HCSB

The enemy would love for this not to be true. He'd rejoice to fool us into believing we can only experience God's presence by happenstance, if we experience Him at all. But if we are indwelt by the Living God, then we carry His presence everywhere we go. And it is not necessary that we *feel* Him in order to present His Life in us; it is our reality. And in this reality, we should expect the landscape of our world to change. It is a matter of faith! You are bringing in the King of Glory and nothing can remain the same in the Light of His Life.

Belief is key in this. When we have faith in Christ's living presence, then we manifest His Life in our world. But if we go into situations asking for His presence, that's unbelief in His Life in us NOW. It takes faith and belief because unbelief quenches the Spirit.

I am not saying that God will not be present without my belief, because He is always present. But doubt will cause us to miss experiencing Him. We can expect His presence *as fact*. We can enter our life, filled with the faith that He *IS* present, *because He is*. When you come into a situation *in* Christ, you know that you come in His authority and with the full weight of God behind you. You are a living minister and ambassador of His presence. This is true of every indwelt child of God.

Whether at the store or in the sanctuary, Christ's Life affects *everyone*, not just the spiritual. You can be a servant of the King of Glory and usher Him in to every situation. And I mean every situation! If you stand in the pleasing faith that you are a living ark of His presence, then you can watch to see how His presence will color your world. No one need know. God often is a Secret-Squirrel-agent of becoming. You can stand next to a person knowing that the Lord of the universe is affecting everything in them. They leave the encounter changed, even if they are not conscious of what happened. But again, this takes faith in the reality of Christ's indwelling.

Often I have walked through my world trusting more in my lack than His fullness. I pray for His filling rather than believing in His fullness. Do you see the difference? One is asking for what I already have, the other is proceeding with faith that I have been filled. I enter any circumstance and bring in His Lordship with *that* faith. The key is faith and belief; unbelief only thwarts this from happening.

I wrote this affirmation some time ago: "I am the fullness of God because God's fullness dwells in me!" Faith in this reality makes me an usher of His Holy presence and a continual presenter of the Creator of Life, life's Redeemer.

And you are in Him, made full and having come to fullness of life [in Christ you too are filled with the Godhead—Father, Son and Holy Spirit—and reach full spiritual stature]. And He is the Head of all rule and authority [of every angelic principality and power].
Colossians 2:10 AMPC

I Am the Dwelling of God

I am not sure that we have a true appreciation for how God views holiness, so let's continue to look at the Ark of the Covenant. No one in their right mind would have abused God's Holy Ark. His Seat of Mercy was to be handled with utmost respect and reverent care. Even the secular world knows this.

Watch the movie *Raiders of the Lost Ark* and see what happened to the Nazis who even dared to look inside. Or look at what happened to Uzzah, a servant of King David assisting in returning the Ark of the Covenant to Jerusalem. He dropped dead for merely attempting to steady the Ark from falling off of the cart. Was not this a good deed, done with the best intentions? Maybe so, but he died for daring to touch the dwelling of the Lord *even with his good intentions.*

Why was utter reverence so important to God? Because it was **His** chosen dwelling place. The Ark was absolutely HOLY! It contained the Testimony of God for His people, Israel.

Let's look at another tabernacle of God's chosen dwelling place — US. How many of us trash this dwelling, sometimes daily? Yes, we are His chosen dwellings. Each of us is a living tabernacle, holy like the ancient Tabernacle that held the Ark of the Covenant. But most of us have no qualms about punching, kicking, or trashing ourselves. We judge ourselves, criticize ourselves, and abuse ourselves with not even the remotest hesitation.

Are we or are we not the dwelling place of the Lord? Doesn't He now live in our hearts, by His own choice? If we are born from above, He now resides in our bodies - and we are a living tabernacle. He has made Himself at home in our hearts, and our lives are a testimony of His grace and love.

You are our epistle written in our hearts, known and read by all men; clearly you are an epistle of Christ, ministered by us, written not with ink but by the Spirit of the living God, not on tablets of stone but on tablets of flesh, that is, of the heart.
2 Corinthians 3:2-3 NKJV

If I am the chosen dwelling place of God, how dare I scorn or revile ME, His choice? Regardless of how I view my worthiness or worthlessness, I ***am*** God's choice. Yes, me. And YOU! We have no right to abuse His home in any way, on any day.

The Old Testament priests handled the Holy Ark with honor, respect, and reverence. They followed God's instructions exactly. The Tabernacle was set up in God's perfect order. And His glory dwelt in the Tabernacle and then in the Temple. The severest consequences were issued for not reverencing God's dwelling, and so the Israelis did.

But Now, you are His dwelling. The Lord indwells you and your life carries His testimony. Your new heart and new life is a creative miracle. Christ came to rend the veil between man and God. His presence left the Tabernacle/Temple and now He resides in you. And as the chosen dwelling of the Lord, you must value, reverence, and honor yourself.

We have no right to indulge self-hatred, self-bitterness, unforgiveness of self, criticism of yourself, calling yourself stupid, raging or fostering anger against ourselves. You are the living tabernacle of God. Your life is a tent of meeting where He chooses to commune with you. You must treat yourself with as much respect as you would have that the ancient Tabernacle and Ark of the Covenant. This is not an option; this is God's requirement.

Or do you not know that your body is a temple of the Holy Spirit within you, whom you have from God? You are not your own, for you were bought with a price. So glorify God in your body.
1 Corinthians 6:19-20 ESV

Do You Mean That's About ME?

When reading the Scripture and its promises, I have often struggled with claiming those promises as my own. Wielding the Word as a personal weapon of acquisition never seemed altogether genuine to me. I am not talking about the obvious scriptures for the church, the Bride, and the disciples of Christ, but the ones clearly assigned to Christ and Israel. It felt odd because the messianic scriptures are for and about Jesus and not me, right? Wrong! They *are* about me.

This is not entitlement or the presumption like a spoiled child. The promises are about me, because I am *in Him*. Some of you may say, "But of course!" But for me, this revelation is huge.

God is calling forth the Life of the Son from your clay-made-vessel, your being, and your life. The joy of this is that now these messianic scriptures are for and fulfilled by Christ in you. The Father is literally calling forth Christ's fulfilling of His own requirements in you. This opens the whole of the scriptures to me. It has always been a love letter *to* me, but now it is about His fulfilling Life and promise *through* me.

2 Corinthians 1:20 says, *"All the promises of God find their Yes in Him [Christ]. That is why it is through Him that we utter our Amen to God for His glory."* It is obvious that all the promises of scripture find their fulfillment in Christ. And as we are in Christ and Christ's Life is in us, we see their fulfillment through us.

> *The Spirit of the Lord God is upon me, because the Lord has anointed me to bring good news to the poor; he has sent me to bind up the brokenhearted, to proclaim liberty to the captives, and the opening of the prison to those who are bound; to proclaim the*

year of the Lord's favor, and the day of vengeance of our God; to comfort all who mourn...
Isaiah 61:1-2 ESV

I have heard many speak this scripture as if it were about themselves. It was their Gospel mandate and they claimed it as their own promise. Now this is clearly a messianic scripture and its reality is found in Christ. In actuality, the only way this is about *me* is when it is about *Christ in me*. His Life brings the Good News, not mine.

Jesus binds up the brokenhearted and proclaims liberty to the captives, not me. But He can do all of this *through me*. Jesus lives out His provisions, His promises, and yes, even His prophecies through me.

Scripture speaks of God's design, plans, and intentions for this world. So many of His promises were fulfilled while He walked the earth. But in our times, in these last days, Jesus lives His Life through us. Not my life, ***His***. Jesus satisfies the Father through us and in us. Thank you, Jesus!

Roles of Life

We have many roles and hats that we wear each and every day. We are parents, teachers, sons and daughters, pastors, cops, doctors, spouses, and the list goes on and on. Living life is about doing as much as being. As we live life, we live out our various roles and callings. But is it me or Jesus that must be these roles?

I contend that every role ascribed to me, from son to shepherd to artist to minister is a role and assignment for Jesus, not me. Are you a husband or wife? It is Christ who intends to live out your life with your spouse. He is to be the husband to your wife, and the wife for your husband. Do I have brothers or sisters? Jesus desires to be the brother to my siblings. This is simply amazing.

This is made very evident in the holiday seasons, when all our roles are called to the fore. During the holidays, most of us have family pulling us in, and it is the Lord who wants to meet them in me. He wants to interact through me, *as me*. I get the opportunity to witness Him in me interacting with the people I love. I get the privilege of knowing Christ ever more deeply as He performs my life and relationships. My desired nearness to Jesus is brought about as I witness Him walk the earth within me.

Even when I take a vacation, Jesus wants to live out that time through me. My rest is still about Him, not me. He is my life in totality and He is the living out of my life. I cannot say that I am an expert in this, but it is my choice. Even my inability to live the Exchanged Life is His to face, not mine.

What then stands between me and experiencing Christ in me? It is my preference for self over Him. If my desire is to know Him above all other knowledge, I will give Him the preeminence. He will have the position to perform while I witness.

Do I desire to experience Jesus in my vacation or am I just trying to take a break for myself? It is not as if Jesus doesn't want me to have rest. The Exchanged Life is all about rest. If I seek the adventure of knowing Him in my holiday, I will experience Him. It is all about preference and His Will. My life is always about my will; His life is always about His.

I am choosing to witness Jesus' Will and Life rather than mine. I want to know more of who He is as opposed to what I feel, think or am. There is no real mystery to me, my life, or my happenings. Since we all have sinned and continually fall short of the glory of God (Romans 3:23), mankind is dull. But Christ in me is all fascination and wonder. As I watch Him do what I am completely incapable of doing, I love Him more. I feel near to Him because Jesus *is me*. I heard someone say, "You cannot be closer to someone than for two to live in one body." This is so true!

I Find Power in My Weakness

Our utter dependence on Christ is one of our *greatest* gifts. While it frustrates our flesh, offends our pride, and hurts our feelings, it is the making of us. As we live in this world, weakness is our greatest strength. Imagine, the only strength we have to affect life is through our weakness! Life lived out of weakness is the only power to show goodness and godliness through our lives.

I can look at your life and see areas you might need to change and you can do the same for me, but changes made from these *opinions* do not make a happier life. Even if I did everything "correctly" I still would not experience God or godliness. Christ's Life is our only answer, and His answer is only achieved through our dependence and weakness.

What if I stopped living life in my best effort and instead embraced my weakness? I would experience *real* Life. How can this be? Because Life erupts from weakness not out of strength.

The Apostle Paul said, "Therefore I will boast all the more gladly of my weaknesses, so that the power of Christ may rest upon me" (2 Cor. 12:9). Some versions say "**glory** in my weakness." Paul came to the place where weakness was something to celebrate not resist. And there is only one reason why he would celebrate his weakness…because Christ Himself would be Paul's Life and strength. This is the position in which we are all intended to live. **Weakness is our strength!**

This takes the pressure of performance off my plate and allows me to settle into *reliance*. Oh, I love that word. Reliance is living with Christ's Life as my life. The only work I must perform, which is the greatest of all works, is just to believe. Our faith is in His Life while we live weak and void of self-strength.

How do you do this? The Word says that we reckon ourselves dead. To reckon is a mathematical term of fact. It is an accounting term. 2+2 has always equaled 4, regardless of any worldly condition or factor. This is the way God-through-Paul called us to view our self-life—counted as DEAD, a mathematical fact. This is also how we embrace our weakness. Christ is my strength *because I am dead.*

We are Weak, but He is Strong

Like most men, I was not born with an innate appreciation for weakness. When I was a little boy, we sang the song called *Jesus Loves Me*. And there was a line in that song that I did not like to sing: **"They are weak, but He is strong!"** Perhaps I just did not want to be that vulnerable to anything or anyone. I came by this honestly; our parents Adam and Eve did not like this state of being much either. But my life's calling has always been to my weakness. That is where God calls me to stay. It feels a little like being asked to run a marathon as a paralytic.

So why would God do this to me? God wants to shine in the very area of my total deficit. And not only does He want to be the Life in that place, He has tied my destiny to His *performing* of it. To win my race, I must lean on Him to run it, for I have no ability to achieve it on my own.

Why on earth would God not build upon my strengths and abilities? He made me with them, so why not use them as a launching pad? Well, quite frankly, it is because in these areas I have pride and the greatest self-sufficiency. I would end up boasting in my ability.

As I touched on earlier, the areas of our greatest weakness – which are often the places we've been most wounded – are where Jesus desires to bring forth His amazing resurrected life. He lives His life out of my complete deficit. Where I have no ability and more, where my performance is a *liability*, that's where Jesus is strongest. My failure is merely the stage where His Life shines more brightly.

Who is weak without my feeling that weakness? Who is led astray, and I do not burn with anger? If I must boast, I would rather boast about the things that show how weak I am.
2 Corinthians 11:29-30 NLT

My dependence is His desire, and He underlines its importance by tying my eternal destiny to it. God calls us to be what I have no ability to be! You could look at this the wrong way and think that it is cruel. But not only is it not cruel, it is His tremendous faithfulness. Our Lord knows the danger of our independence. He binds us to the need of Him on a molecular level. He knows that we cannot truly survive within the walls of self. We cannot sustain a self-life and expect an eternal one *with Him*. He is faithful to set us up for the greatest eternal reward—Himself.

But He said to me, "My grace is sufficient for you, for My power is made perfect in weakness." Therefore I will boast all the more gladly about my weaknesses, so that Christ's power may rest on me.
2 Corinthians 12:9 NIV

Trying to Live It Out in the Soul

Because Christ came and gave us everything we need for Life and godliness, He now requires His Provision to be used. The indwelling Christ gave me something nothing else could: the actual Life to perform the Will of God. Jesus is not just saying, "Hey you, this is what I want, now go and do it!" No, Jesus Christ has not only *made* the way, He **is** the Way. His Life is my performance.

This is foreign to most, I know it was for me. I thought the Will of God was just about what God required of me and wanted me to do. On the contrary, God's expectations are on the Life of His Son, not *my* effort to perform. Christ's Life *is* my life, so all effort is blasphemy.

"Blasphemy is a mighty strong word there, John!" Yes, it is, so why would I use it to describe our efforts? The first and most important reason is because that is what I heard our Heavenly Father say to me: "Effort is blasphemy!"

The second reason is because blasphemy perfectly describes the offense. "*Blasphemy is the act of insulting or showing contempt or lack of reverence to a deity, to religious or holy persons or sacred things, or toward something considered sacred or inviolable.*"

Effort is trust and faith in my own performance rather than Christ's. Now that the actual Life of Jesus Christ has been given to me, it is truly foolish to continue my efforts. Above foolish, it is an affront to my God who gave me that which pleases Him—Christ Himself.

It is very much like being given everything I need to get a job done, yet choosing to scrounge through a dumpster looking for tools instead. How contemptuous of God's gift!

Remember:

Christ's life as my life
is His Life in my life,
and that's not my life as His Life,
it is HIM.

We must always come with the Life of the Spirit in the Will of God. We must not only do the Will of God but also do it His way. If we do the Will of God in the soul, we are in as much rebellion as if we had never done His Will at all. The Will of God and the Life of God are one *or it is rebellion, period.* There is no distinction between the Will and the Life. The Life of Christ ***is*** the Will of God.

I've seen many over the years who heard the Will of God, and then performed it themselves. This left a huge trail of tears. The fruit of my own life and effort is death, even when it seems helpful or productive. Only Christ's Life can perform God's Will. The goal is not the completion of a task; it is the Life Source. Jesus wants to be *the* Doer of all our doing.

Our spiritual passion, zeal, and ambition should never be the fuel propelling our life. And even knowing the Will of God is no substitute for letting His Life perform it. Just because we know what He wants to do doesn't give us the right to run ahead of Him to do it. Remember Moses?

In the course of time Moses grew up. Then he went to see his own people and watched them suffering under forced labor. He saw a Hebrew, one of his own people, being beaten by an Egyptian. He looked all around, and when he did not see anyone, he beat the Egyptian to death and hid the body in the sand.

When Moses went there the next day, he saw two Hebrew men fighting. He asked the one who started the fight, "Why are you beating another Hebrew?" The man asked, "Who made you our ruler and judge? Are you going to kill me as you killed the Egyptian?"

Then Moses was afraid and thought that everyone knew what he had done. When Pharaoh heard what Moses had done, he tried to have him killed. But Moses fled from Pharaoh and settled in the land of Midian.
Exodus 2:11-15 GW

Moses, who was called by God to lead Israel out of slavery, took it upon himself to perform this calling under his own strength—and became a murderer. We, too, bring death with our performance of God's Will.

There is nothing to substitute for the actual Life of Christ. *Nothing.* Again, the movement of the Spirit and the Will of God come from the Life of Christ. Simply hearing the Will of God does not give me a green light to proceed. **Timing is subject to the Life of Christ Who performs the Will of God.** Jesus paid a high price for me to have His Life, so I say yes for Him to live it through me!

When Do I Move?

Having established that the Life of Christ is the Will of God, what do I do if the Spirit is prompting me to do something? It means He wants to move on it. I have missed opportunities by waiting mere minutes for it to be more convenient. The Spirit knows what I do not and His timing is ALWAYS perfect. I am to strike while the iron is hot!

Recently the Spirit urged me to record a video with Martha Kilpatrick. We knew we were supposed to do one but we were waiting on the timing. The Spirit moved while I was driving but I thought, "I will just get us home and we can do it then." By the time we got there though, His *fire* had dissipated, which made it more difficult. And although God had mercy on us and allowed us to do the video, it was not perfect. We had to do a number of takes and it was stressful. The Holy Spirit knew something but my *logic* thought it knew better.

The Spirit of God is *GOD* of my moments. He knows things outside my purview, and even beyond that, His Will is my life. As I walk this Life in Him, I have to be utterly surrendered to His Spirit, never leaning on my logic. Logic will fool you. Why? Because logic is the mind of the flesh and is completely incompatible with the Will of God! More than incompatible, it *always* thinks it knows better than God because it is fueled by Satan.

We all should walk in reverence, as our every moment is holy. When we belong to the Father, and Christ's Life is our life, we dwell in His Will. This means God dictates our every where, when, what, and how. This is both freeing and frightening. Frightening because we do have access to a nature that prefers our mind over the Will of God. Freeing because as I walk yielded to Him, I am released from the striving of my flesh. His Life is peace, while logic is a cruel mistress!

I do not want to let the mind of my flesh have even the smallest leeway. My logic enthrones Satan and gives him permission to bring chaos and death.

Our temptation usually is to focus on expediting tasks, making them serve our goals rather than surrendering to and living in God's Will. It happens in the most minute of circumstances, but it has eternal significance. My choice is surrender! I desire to bring forth His Life, to strike while the iron is hot—not follow my logic and will. Will you stand with me in this?

When I come up against the Law I want to do good, but in practice I do evil. My conscious mind whole-heartedly endorses the Law, yet I observe an entirely different principle at work in my nature. This is in continual conflict with my conscious attitude, and makes me an unwilling prisoner to the law of sin and death.

In my mind I am God's willing servant, but in my own nature I am bound fast, as I say, to the law of sin and death. It is an agonizing situation, and who on earth can set me free from the clutches of my sinful nature? I thank God there is a way out through Jesus Christ our Lord.
Romans 7:21-25 Phillips

Waiting for the Right Timing

You may be experiencing some confusion after reading the last two chapters. First I told you that knowing God's Will does not mean that you can presume to move on it immediately. And then I said that when the Holy Spirit moves on something, we are to move with Him. How do we reconcile this seeming contradiction? The Life of Christ.

God alone determines the timing of the move of the Life of Christ in me. God lets His children in on *what* He is doing, but this doesn't mean that we know *how* or *when*. Look at Christ's return. We know neither the day nor the hour but as His children, we are privy to the season. While I cannot *make* Christ return, I know that He is returning, because He said He would. God's Ways and timing is always His to reveal.

When the Spirit is moving in me, it is the Life of Christ moving in me. So, I strike when the iron is hot. He moves and I move; we move together in tandem and I get to watch His Life in me. This is very different from presuming on the Will of God. The soul will trick us, tempting us to run ahead of the Life of Christ. "I *know*, so therefore I *do*!" But that is not how it works.

There is a process of death and resurrection in the Exchanged Life. The wind of the Spirit blows where it wills and this makes us utterly dependent on Him. The Lord may tell me His Will, yet not move on it in that moment. He might be inviting me to pray, to wait with Him for His timing, or just to stand in faith. I must follow, not direct, His Life as He lives it through me. This is a daily cross, and this is my death. But it is also a delight if I see all of my life in light of knowing Him – and not just getting things done.

My urgency is never His directive, and my zeal does not determine His timing. The Spirit of Christ looks for my agreement, and then often requires my surrender to reveal His timing. God determines when His Life will manifest, both when He strikes and when He waits in me.

If I am motivated to please God, then my knowing His Will builds excitement not ambition. If I start to fret, then I am clearly prioritizing my will over His. Zeal, joy, and excitement precipitate His Will. Even when that Will is judgment, there is an excitement for the Lord revealing Himself.

Remember, this Life is about His Life in me. As I always say, "Christ's life as my life is His life in my life, and that's not my life as His life, *it is HIM*." Jesus is in control of the Life and the expression of His Will. And if we will choose to surrender rather than presume, we will discover that the Lord's timing is always best.

> *For My thoughts are not your thoughts, neither are your ways My ways, says the Lord. For as the heavens are higher than the earth, so are My ways higher than your ways and My thoughts than your thoughts.*
> Isaiah 55:8-9 AMPC

My Best Really Isn't Good Enough in The Great Exchange

Our job in this life is not to go off on our own and get busy, busy, busy, work, work, work, trying in vain to produce fruit. Trying to love people on our own will lead to a life of frustration. Our responsibility is not to produce the fruit of the Spirit on our own. Our responsibility is to have a relationship to Jesus Christ and to let God use us. It is a life yielded to Christ. It is a life of rest.

J. Delany
(Pastor of Salem Bible Church in Salem, NH)

Christian living is not a method or technique. It is the principle of an exchanged Life.

Major Ian Thomas
(evangelist, writer, teacher and founder of Torchbearers Bible schools 1914-2007)

But I'm Doing My BEST!

"I'm doing my best!" I think we've all heard that before, and most of us have said it a time or two as well. Sadly, I have some really bad news. **Your best is not good enough.** Neither is mine, and it *never will be.*

The fruits of doing our best are frustration, bitterness, anger, exhaustion, and depression, to name a few. Think about when you usually hear someone say, "I'm doing my best!" Is it delivered in joy or contentment? No, it is usually whipped out like a defense, paired with another common phrase: "What do you want from me?!" Deep inside we all know that our best is not good enough.

This life is a continual process of proving that we cannot do it on our own. As evidenced in our first parents (Adam and Eve), and then illustrated painfully throughout the Old Testament, we really cannot do it. We can do none of it! We were never designed to manhandle this life on our own.

A particular abuse is perpetrated on children around the world: Parents give their child the responsibility to manage their little lives on their own. Such irresponsibility! These parents neglect to actually parent, which is abusive. It is abusive because it heaps on the child a weight they cannot carry. Yet our Heavenly Father does not do this to His children. He truly parents us by not only directing us, but also giving us the Life that can perform those directions.

The Lord has no expectations of ME; He expects only from the Life of His Son. Our best will never get me over the threshold into Holiness. "Good" behavior possibly, but not the Life of Christ. Bad fruit cannot come from a Good Tree, and Good Fruit cannot come from a bad tree. Our self-life is just a bad tree with bad fruit. Sure, we might be able to polish up and wax our fruit to make it appear good in the moment, but with one bite, the rotten core would be revealed. Our obsessive-compulsive demand that we be Christ-like without His Life is nothing but foolishness – and a huge insult to God.

As God told me so clearly, effort is blasphemy. And our effort is blasphemy because it feeds the original lies Satan told Eve in the Garden: "You don't have what you need, God doesn't care about you, and there are no consequences for living independently of Him." Those lies still live in our flesh today.

Whenever I am not willing to wait on His Life to move, I'm blasphemously trying my best *independently of God*. But my self-life is not Christ's Life *even if I get the job done*. What we do through effort is DEATH, bad fruit from a bad tree. What Jesus does, no matter how small, is eternal, and LIFE.

> *I have been crucified with Christ; and it is no longer I who live, but Christ lives in me; and the life which I now live in the flesh I live by faith in the Son of God, who loved me and gave Himself up for me.*
> Galatians 2:20 NASB

The truth is that Christ's Life is the *only* satisfactory life to our Father and Creator. And because God is good, when we are born-again, the Life of the Son of God is available to us—NOW. So my best is not good enough, and it does not need to be. Jesus is THE Best, and He lives in me.

> *While he was still speaking, a bright cloud overshadowed them, and behold, a voice out of the cloud said, "This is My beloved Son, with whom I am well-pleased; listen to Him!" When the disciples heard this, they fell face down to the ground and were terrified.*
> Matthew 17:5-6 NASB

Being a Radical for Christ

The drive to give God our best is all too normal in the Christian world. A while back I read *The Irresistible Revolution: Living as an Ordinary Radical* by Shane Claiborne, a man who got out of his pew and went off in search of the life Jesus experienced. He wanted to know true, authentic Christianity. Claiborne was on a crusade, and in his search, he even went to Calcutta to visit Mother Teresa and work with the Sisters of Mercy for a summer.

This man worked to be Jesus with skin on, a phrase I have heard many times. Claiborne's hope was to be the hands and feet of Jesus, to live out the scripture, "It is no longer I who live, but Christ lives in me." This all sounds well and good, and I did enjoy reading his stories. Yet nowhere in this book did Claiborne mention Christ's mind. If it were truly "*not I but Christ*" then his functioning would be under the mind of Jesus.

I am not trying to unduly criticize Claiborne. He is actually getting out there while thousands of others sit lifeless in the pews. But excessive action is not what makes a life godly.

Claiborne said, "Rather than waiting around for God's special plan for your life, you should just go where God is at work and join in." There is a prevalent error at work in this statement and it affects the Exchanged Life we are called to live.

The social gospel is alive and well. Feed the hungry, heal the leper, and turn the other cheek. "Find a need and pick it up and then all day you'll have good luck." The error is introduced when this social gospel is propelled by *my* life and assumed goodness. We are not called to supply the needs of the world as we see them; we are called to let Christ live our lives. This is what "***not I but Christ***" means. *It is not my life*—it is His.

You might say, "But John, there are thousands and thousands of hungry and even starving people out there!" Yes, and yet my calling is not to meet man's need with my own supply; I am to listen to the Provider and allow Him to supply *His need*. Talk about revolution, if we all lived like *that*, we would have a radical existence indeed! A true radical in Christ follows the lead of Christ's Life.

I am concerned about any movement that utilizes the strength of youth to perpetuate a social gospel. This path ends in weary, worn-out, disillusioned, and embittered saints. If we are attempting to live Christ's life in our own strength and under our own compulsion, we *will* break under the unsustainable weight.

And thank God that we do break! God never intended for *my* strength and zeal to perform good Christian deeds. The Spirit of the Living God is able to communicate His mind and will toward an enormously needy, broken world quite sufficiently without my input.

The social gospel is easy; it requires nothing but my motivation to do. I decide, I perform, and it is done. Surrendering to the mind of Christ is difficult. Christ in me can be nebulous. He is a mystery. And His is the **only** Life that pleases the Father and can truly, even *radically* minister to this lost world.

Then suddenly the voice of the Father shouted from the sky, saying, "This is the Son I love, and my greatest delight is in Him."
Matthew 3:17 TPT

The Doing of the Doers

I come from a long line of doers, but being a doer is not necessarily a problem; the problem is the *source* of my doing. Who is behind all my doing, God or me?

We can run ourselves ragged being a doer. And many things can fuel this activity. Here are a few examples:

- **Bitterroot judgment**: "I won't be lazy like…"
- **Earning love**: working hard to gain love or approval.
- **Competition**: working hard to prove you're better than someone else.
- **Compensation**: slaving to overcome feelings of worthlessness.
- **The outright workaholic**: just trying to BE something or someone.
- **Crazy workhorse**: working to avoid something or someone painful.

Work is highly subjective and deeply emotional. If you are not a drone and are a bit driven…there is probably something behind it.

I have given a list of reasons driving our work, but there is actually only one real work we are called to do. It is the work to hear and believe. Yes, the doing of doers should be about the work of hearing and believing more than doing. All doing should emanate from a place of hearing, not simply doing. Doers that are not hearers are actually lazy. They do not think that they are lazy, because they are continually doing, but they are.

"Activity suggests a life filled with purpose."
Capt. Von Trapp, *The Sound of Music*

Many people agree with Von Trapp, but the real work of this life is the work of hearing and believing, not the chaotic flailing of mere activity.

So Jesus explained, "I tell you the truth, the Son can do nothing by Himself. He does only what He sees the Father doing. Whatever the Father does, the Son also does.
John 5:19 NLT

Anyone can preoccupy themselves with doing. Being a doer is simple. A life of activity does not prove purpose; it only proves action. And busy movement can fool us. This exerted energy feels anything but lazy. "Lazy is sedentary, *right*?" No, laziness is purposelessness. Activity proves nothing because effort is not eternal unless it is sourced in God. Purpose is only found in the Life of Christ in me. And this is achieved only through hearing and believing.

Jesus told them, "This is the only work God wants from you: Believe in the One He has sent."
John 6:29 NLT

All our doing must be sourced in Christ's Life and His performance. Our true work is found in hearing and believing Him, not in doing the actual job. It has to be more than hearing; it has to become believing or you have not heard.

Hearing and believing are a living activity.

Therefore everyone who hears these words of Mine and acts on them is like a wise man who built his house on the rock.
Matthew 7:24 NIV

Facing the Despair of the Great Exchange

As you accept the reality that Christ's Life alone pleases God, you may find yourself in the depths of despair. And that is NOT a problem! Not only did Christ give His followers reason to rejoice, He also continually gave them cause for despair. Walking with Him must have been the most exciting and horrifying thing ever—like a rollercoaster for the soul. Whenever those with Him thought they *"had it,"* He would purposely douse their confidence. He made sure that they knew salvation is not an acquisition; it is a Person. Salvation is *in Jesus,* and by no other means are men saved.

We live in perpetual dependence on Jesus Christ. It makes *most* of us quiver with despair to know that we are that dependent on Him, while the rest just pretend that it is not true. In looking at those who walked physically with Jesus, we see the evidence of their quandary displayed in their questions and every interaction with Him. Here are merely two examples in the Gospels.

*Those who heard this asked, "**Who then** can be saved?"*
Jesus replied, "What is impossible with man is possible with God."
Luke 18:26-27 NIV

*This made them ask Him, "**What must we do** to carry*
out the work of God?"
"The work of God for you," replied Jesus, "is to believe in the One
whom He has sent to you."
John 6:28-29 Phillips

"What must we do?" This question sounds desperate to me. Jesus answers with, "You must believe that I can and will do it!" These scriptures show the disciples' despair and Jesus' response to that despair: "It is in Me!" He proclaims, "It's impossible for you, do you hear Me? It IS impossible. But with God ALL things are possible!"

Our despair is the continual reminder that we must have His Life. We must have Another's Life to perform our life. "WHO CAN BE SAVED?" and "WHAT MUST I DO?" are the desperate cries of people in need of Christ's Life, His salvation and His Person as the Answer.

Our deep despair over not being able to perform is both an invitation to lean into Christ's Life as well as a check that I am probably kicking against the goads. If I am the only one out there finding it difficult to get my tasks done, then I speak this to myself. But if you, like me, struggle in the despair that no matter how hard you try, you cannot get things done, then you're in luck. The despair is evidence of God's call for you to relinquish your efforts, because it truly is impossible. It is also a reminder to believe that He makes all things possible.

His Life is the only life. We are actually supposed to rub against the despair of life. This is the only way we learn of our inability and utter dependence on Him. When the enemy tempts us towards discouragement, anger with God and unbelief, Jesus says, "I am your Way, I am your Life, and I make all things possible. *Just believe*."

Jesus looked steadily at them and replied, "Humanly speaking it is impossible; but with God anything is possible!"
Matthew 19:26 PHILLIPS

*For you are saved by grace through faith, and this is **not** from yourselves; it is God's gift—**not** from works, so that no one can boast.*
Ephesians 2:8-9 HCSB

Live Listening, Not Knowing

I am now going to share a major secret of how to live without effort and trying. Ready? Live your life *listening*, not *knowing*.

I saw this clearly while working with a friend and brother who functions the same way; he lives listening, not knowing. When I live with the great "I know," I thwart my ability to hear God. Knowing is deafness to His telling. When I go into any situation *knowing* what is to be done, I am not positioning my heart to hear the Lord's direction. Knowing is telling, not listening or *hearing*. This is a travesty because it prevents me from enjoying His Life.

Jesus said to them, "I assure you that the Son can do nothing of His own accord, but only what He sees the Father doing.
John 5:19 PHILLIPS

Christ lived His Life listening to His Father. He did nothing that He did not first see the Father doing. All that Jesus did was through listening, NOT knowing. And today He wants to do the same through me.

Life is not about listening to *do*, per se; it is listening to activate my volitional will in order to be surrendered to *His* Will and Life. He wants my will yielded to His Will by choosing His Will, not performing it. Remember: "Christ's life as my life is **His** life in *my* life, and that's not my life as His life, it's HIM." My attentiveness to His voice by listening-not-knowing is for surrender, agreement, and volition – not doing. He is the Doer and I am the listener. I hear *what* He wants to do and *how* He wants to do it. And then HE does it.

When I transferred our ministry's web server to a new host, I experienced this in living color. The main work of the transfer was complete and it looked like it was all ease and friendliness. I even posted on Facebook before going to bed to thank everyone for praying. It looked like the smoothest transition ever. But at 4 AM the next morning, I was quantifiably shown to be wrong. When I checked everything, it was all upside down. I was at a complete loss. I had no idea what to do! I just sat there, mind running a million miles an hour, trying to figure it out. "Who do I call? What do I do? WHERE DO I START?"

"STEP AWAY FROM THE WEBSITES!"

I had to leave it all because I started in with a load of potential solutions when I needed nothing but His Voice and Will. In the thick of the mayhem, I actually had to shut down my computer, get in the car, and drive to a place I could park and stare. This is so completely counter to my nature, by the way. I fix things. I'm a hands-on fixer!

When I came back, I had a new sense of purpose because I had listened and *heard*. I was able to systematically dismantle the problems. And when I needed a running mate, my friend jumped in with the same listening-not-knowing approach. This is not an anomaly; this is what Jesus intends for us. Christ lived this way when He walked the earth, and He wishes to live this way in us today.

Looking to Be Faithful

Humanity's desire to produce something of worth within ourselves is as tenacious as it is futile. I recently saw a church marquee which read, "Our God is Always Faithful – Are We?" Everything in my body erupted with a resounding, "NO! And that's the point!" Now, I have no idea what message this pastor was to deliver in connection to this sign. It might have been spot on. But for most of the passers-by, it conveyed this message: "Buck up, buddy! Do your part." How deflating and defeating. We cannot, and that is the entire point of the Exchanged Life.

I would love to tell you that I, in myself, am a shining beacon of faithfulness. After all, look at all that God has done for me. Should not I be able to at least devote myself by towing the line and keeping up my end of the deal? Only in the land of make-believe. We live in a fallen world, one where we are utterly dependent, not dependable. This is the land where we *epically* fail apart from God.

But this is exciting! We are completely reliant on Another to enact His own requirements of our lives. We have been let off the performance hook, while being completely responsible to choose His performance. So what is the answer when the marquee asks, "Our God is Always Faithful – Are We?" Emphatically, no! And why? God IS faithful and we ARE NOT, but *He* is our faithfulness! This is the purpose of our entire lives. And those who receive that, rejoice.

That sign could have read, "God is always faithful. Thank God He lives His faithfulness out through us!" Our fear of failure and rejection is solved by Christ's Life. His Life as my life is a reality. We died in His crucifixion and He, not I, was resurrected. This is the intended exchange, the *great* Exchange.

Our God is always faithful — are we? Yes, we are more than conquerors ***IN Christ***. He is my life, my faithfulness, and my ever-faithful God!

If we are faithless, He remains faithful — for He cannot deny Himself.
2 Timothy 2:13 ESV

Your Heart and Intentions

Because He is faithful, God waits for our choice and our intention. Straight from our hearts, He is looking for our purposed direction, rather than our performance. Throughout the Old Testament, He showed again and again that performance is not possible from the created, only by the Creator.

It is debilitating to be required to perform a task and have no ability to do it. Imagine if your boss set forth an impossible task and said to you, "If you don't do this, **you're fired**!" Some of us would just sit down and cry, while others might put in a fighting effort, but it has already been determined that the task is impossible. Well, the Holy Life is the same. Righteousness is God's to perform alone.

Our God has a holy standard we are all required to meet. None of us are exempt, and failure to meet it requires death as atonement. In the Old Testament, it was the death of bulls and goats. And in the New Testament, Christ the Redeemer is our Living Sacrifice. But death has always been the only satisfaction for failing to meet the requirements of the Law. Praise God He gave us Himself as the Solution! Yet He still yearns for our intention to be displayed. It reveals to us and to Him the direction of our heart. It is the faith that pleases Him.

The Intention of Abraham

God asked Abraham to sacrifice his beloved son, Isaac, on top of Mount Moriah. Mount Moriah is the mountain that the modern day Temple Mount sits upon. But the actual top of that mountain is located further north of the Temple Mount, another 90 feet higher. The peak of Mount Moriah is a place we now call Golgotha. This is the very place that our Heavenly Father sacrificed His only begotten Son on the Cross. Yes, at the very place where God asked

Abraham to express his intentions by connecting his heart to an act of faith, the Father sacrificed His own Son. In Abraham's day, God was looking for Abraham's heart intention and choice of obedience but as a shadow of what God would actually perform IN Jesus. He never was looking for Abraham to perform the act, though he was required to perfectly display his intention.

Intention and Performance

God so longs for our intention towards Him to be revealed. All the while, He loves to be the only performance of His Will and Life. **"Christ's Life as my life is *His Life* in my life, and that's not my life as His life, it's HIM."** God's holiness and righteousness emanates from His very own Life. We've been set free from the slavery and fear of performance and have been given, in the Life of Christ, the power to perform. This is not a strength bestowed upon us to help us to live life but rather Christ's own indwelling Life. Jesus indwells us and lives out His requirements through us!

> *I no longer live, but Christ lives in me. The life I now live in the body, I live by faith in the Son of God, who loved me and gave Himself for me. I do not set aside the grace of God, for if righteousness comes through the law, then Christ died for nothing.*
> Galatians 2:20-21 HCSB

The Difference Between Work and Obedience

God's ideas for your life will always be better than yours. But you do not come to know His idea of your life outside of obedience to His will. Self-will is simply self-enforced structures – rickety buildings of your own making. Yet God's will is a *world* you never knew was possible but always dreamt was true. God's life for you is not stringent, lifeless borders; it is expansive limitless adventures. God's idea of your life, found in the center of His will, is your highest fulfillment and the greatest satisfaction you can know.

Many of us fear that obedience to God means the most difficult, least fun life possible. We think that God's Will means dry oatmeal and sour milk. Well, if God did relegate you to that, I can assure you, you would have His satisfaction in it. God's will requires Christ's Life to perform within His grace. Obedience walked out is the Life of Christ. You choose His will and His Life performs it. This is obedience.

It was no accident that I received the revelation that effort is blasphemy. It was not so I could enlighten others, it was so I would enter into rest. It was an invitation to release the stress of striving. It was convicting *and* liberating. In this light, I want to share the difference between WORK and OBEDIENCE.

Work that emanates from our determined self-life is sin and difficult, whereas obedience to His will is blessed and easy. Christ said that His yoke is easy and His burden is light. When we are struggling and straining in our effort and strength, however, life is anything but easy and light. But Jesus said that *His* yoke is easy and *His* burden is light, not ours. The easy yoke and light burden exists in obedience, not effort. Our effort to do the work is the heavy burden and hard yoke.

His yoke is easy because the Life coming from obedience is easy. Trying to figure things out, remembering what needs to be done, working to find the work is heavy and difficult. All Jesus requires of us is obedience, not WORK. You are not required to plan it all out; you are required to follow moment-by-moment in obedience.

Obedience…not service.
Obedience…not responsibility.
Obedience is Life.

It is amazing that life can be relegated to simple obedience. Listening in this present moment for God's Will. All the anxiety of the future and regrets from the past lose their grip. I just have to say YES in obedience to the Will of the Father. Do you see how that could be easy and light?

But to one who, not working [by the Law], trusts (believes fully) in Him Who justifies the ungodly, his faith is credited to him as righteousness (the standing acceptable to God).
Romans 4:5 AMP

For he who has once entered [God's] rest also has ceased from [the weariness and pain] of human labors, just as God rested from those labors peculiarly His own.
Hebrews 4:10 AMPC

So How Do I Enter The Great Exchange?

The resources of the Christian life, my friends, are just–Jesus Christ… the many references to Christ in you, you in Christ, Christ our life, and abiding in Christ are literal, actual, blessed fact, and not figures of speech… Jesus Christ does not want to be our helper; He wants to be our life. He does not want us to work for Him. He wants us to let Him do His work through us, using us as we use a pencil to write with–better still, using us as one of the fingers of His hand.

Charles C. G. Trumbull
(Influential writer and one of the founders of America's Keswick, 1872-1941*)*

It Is as Easy as YES

In the past, I have believed falsely that this life is hard, that the Christian life and cross life were only a struggle and strain. These old ideas were rooted in my psyche and became a belief system that robbed me of joy. Unfortunately, I know more pinched-faced Christians than joy-filled victors. And I know why that is so! It is because too many do not know how effortless the Christian life can be. Let me tell you what this life requires of you:

"YES!"

That is it, just a yes! How? Because God does not look to my life for performance. *My performance* of His Will is a recipe for destruction. As I have said repeatedly in this book: Christ's life as my life is **His** life *in* my life, and that is not my life as His life, it's Him.

God asks us many things. He comes to us and gives us many choices. But when God says, "I want you to do *so and so,*" He is not conscripting me to go to work; He is asking me for the permission to BE that in me. I have the choice to say yes or no. Where many get hung up – including me from time to time – is the DOING.

Years ago, I heard God's call to singleness, but I could not do that. My attempts to perform this only led to my laws and my failure. I stumbled and fell at every turn. No, my call to celibacy was an invitation to see *Christ* be celibate in me, *through me.*

Let's say you toss a baby into a pool (note: *no babies were hurt in the making of this example*). If that baby has not been trained, they will flail for a moment and then sink to the bottom. But if you have taught that baby to flip over and float, they remain buoyant on top of the water. Well, the Christian life is like the pool, and my efforts to perform this life is a flailing, sinking baby. But my YES to Christ's

Life is like floating buoyant on the waters. Very simplistic visual, I know, but so can the Christian life be.

What if we simply, whole-heartedly opened our lives up to God when He proposed something to us? What if we just heard His voice and said YES? Take anything in your life that God is asking of you. Respond to Him with, "YES, Father, I surrender to Your life to perform that in me. Yes, I want to see that." Now, He is free to accomplish that in you. This is not an exercise in irresponsibility; this is the most responsible thing we can do.

Does that mean I can always escape a painful Gethsemane? That life will never be a struggle for you? No! But Jesus showed us the way. *"Father, if You are willing, please take this cup of suffering away from Me. Yet I want Your will to be done, not Mine"* (Luke 22:42). He said His YES to the Father, and it was God's to perform.

So whether it is a life calling, surrendering to a situation, or developing character, everything God asks of us, He gets to do. EVERYTHING – **except the yes. The YES is ours.**

Accessing All of God

Any place in my life where I have a 'NO' to God only functions to limit His grace and Life.

When I came to Shulamite Ministries I had nothing more than a "YES." I had educational training in nothing, I had experience in nothing, and I had expertise in nothing. I was simply a man with a yes to God, not knowing where or how He would apply that commitment.

With no formal training or even the smallest understanding, I became a computer tech and IT guy, setting up and fixing the many computers of the ministry. I had to be a web developer and maintain our many sites. I became an audio technician, recording and editing all the audio content presented in our Shulamite Podcast and every audio series sold at Living Christian Books. I learned to be a graphic artist and designer, a production and project manager. I was the publicist for Martha Kilpatrick. I have grown into a great travel agent who can stretch a dollar and travel points across the globe and back. I became an awesome farmer and shepherd, succeeding at the art of animal husbandry and veterinary work. I became a builder and general contractor.... This list goes on and on.

And though I may not be doing some of these tasks now, when I was, it was crucial. The administration of the ministry is a one-man show, but that man is not me. Christ's Life has run me through the paces of every step. Jesus is that ONE MAN.

As a city boy, what was I thinking when I found myself elbow deep in the back end of a ewe, assisting in the birth of a breached lamb? What thought crosses my mind when I have to get us to Vienna,

Austria by the end of the week and it is Monday? What passes through my head when the server crashes in the middle of a data transfer, and no tech guy knows why or can even tell me how to fix it? Not much! I do not have the knowledge base to draw from, so it is either Christ's Life or it is nothing.

I say all of this *not* to show how wonderful or capable I am, because I am NOT. I am trying to show you what Christ can do with nothing but a willing YES. I did not place parameters on where I would serve or what I would do, I just said yes. And with that yes came His Life. All the wisdom and understanding I needed to perform these tasks was present with Christ's Life to accomplish them.

I had not locked myself into a role, because a role only limits His Life and the grace to achieve His Will. If I had said, "I am only…" I would have shut God out to being anything other than what I knew to do. "I am only…" is a firm proclamation of the limits of my abilities, my doings and me. So, does this mean I will be required to do things outside of my comfort zone? Absolutely! The horizon is nothing but open – but all to HIM.

"I can do *all things* through Christ who strengthens me," means *anything* Christ wants to do or be in me. Jesus did not call a man of many talents; He called a man with NOTHING. Why? Why would God call an ill-equipped man to start a ministry? It is why He calls any of us who have nothing. He can be everything and this maintains our dependence.

So if you find yourself at a complete loss, behind a mountain of need, rejoice! You are about to see the Life of the King gloriously. He is able when we are not. All Jesus needs is a yes to His will, and then He opens your world to omni-possibilities. Roles and limits only stop Him from being ALL. When I present my life to God as a clean slate, He takes me beyond my life, knowledge and capabilities.

I am ready for anything through the strength of the one who lives within me.
Philippians 4:13 PHILLIPS

Living in My Yes, Not No

The Lord created us all to dwell in the YES rather than a NO. And if I bow to His design of me, then potentiality and possibilities explode.

Increase, expanse, and growth fill The Kingdom. From glory to glory it is exponentially expanding. For the heavens are full of positives, God's amen, the YES and not the NO. And we have the choice to join our Maker in His YES over us. He formed and fashioned you in your mother's womb. He joyfully, *resoundingly* wove you together with YES. Your life's power will always be within your YES to God. This is the way into the Kingdom: a path full of YES to God.

Religion is just a long list of NO's, and there is no life there. We are taught to barricade ourselves within a plethora of NO's in an attempt to become holy. NO to temptation, NO to self, NO to sin, NO to evil desires, and NO to the devil. Yet I am created to live by YES.

For the Son of God, Christ Jesus (the Messiah)…was not Yes and No; but in Him it is [always the **divine***] Yes.*
2 Corinthians 1:19 AMP

My very make-up is shaped for YES, so to structure my life according to a NO leaves me destitute. We cannot live in the power of NO.

Jesus lived *as* a YES to the Father. Even His resistance of Satan in the wilderness was more a statement of His YES to God than His NO to the devil. His refusal of the temptation was a byproduct of His YES to God. Satan's questioning assault was met with an affirmative statement of His YES to God—it was not an "I will not" but an "I will what God wills, as it is written."

For all of God's promises have been fulfilled in Christ
with a resounding "Yes!"
And through Christ, our "Amen" (which means "Yes") ascends
to God for His glory.
2 Corinthians 1:20 NLT

Choose to say YES to God and then your NO will fall in line. God created us in and for YES. He breathed Life into us and that breath was His YES. We, as His creations, bear His mark: YES. Everything is YES and "amen," not NO and "I will not." Life is plus not minus, multiplication not division.

I am His YES. You are His YES. Every fiber of our being is YES and YES holds us together. God's very breath, giving us life, is a Divine YES. His every thought of us is YES. So in response, I say a decisive **YES**!

Our Yeses Merging

For all of God's promises have been fulfilled in Christ
with a resounding "Yes!"
And through Christ, our "Amen" (which means "Yes and Amen")
ascends to God for His glory.
2 Corinthians 1:20 NLT

This is one of the most exciting scriptures. It is the union of my yes to God's Yes, for the purpose of bringing forth His glory. Our affirming God, the Creator of the universe is an explosive YES. His yes is miraculously creative. He said YES to me when I was conceived. YES to my life as I lived. And YES to His Life formed in me. And my only reasonable response is Yes and AMEN.

Here then is the ease of the Christian life: ALL God's promises have been fulfilled in the Life of His Son. They are all YES! And through

Christ, my YES to His promises ascends to God for His glory. Do you see? Oh, this is amazing!

Christ comes and invites me to live in humility. My pride-life *attempts* to be humble—and fails. But when I simply say YES to His Life, Jesus is humility in me, and I get to experience it.

Christ comes and invites me to live in purity. My lustful life attempts to be pure—and fails. But I say YES to Him, and Jesus is purity in me. Jesus calls me to be a pastor. I say YES to Him being a pastor in me, and am able to experience His shepherding through me. One last example. God asks me to leave an unhealthy relationship, and I say YES. I know I cannot do it myself but He can. Christ then works to carry out His will in that relationship.

The divine 'yes' has at last sounded in Him, for in Him is the 'yes' that affirms all the promises of God.
2 Corinthians 1:19-20 Moffatt

Unfortunately, Pain Hurts!

We are hedged in (pressed) on every side [troubled and oppressed in every way], but not cramped or crushed; we suffer embarrassments and are perplexed and unable to find a way out, but not driven to despair;

We are pursued (persecuted and hard driven), but not deserted [to stand alone]; we are struck down to the ground, but never struck out and destroyed...
2 Corinthians 4:8-9 AMPC

God does not put a premium on painless living. What is more, if this is one of your **highest values**, then you will be in direct opposition to Him. I wish I could say that this has never been the case for me, but it used to be. I used to look for whatever would extinguish pain. The good news is that my avoidance of pain did not thwart God from using it, nor stand in the way of Him performing His will in my life. The bad news is that I created additional stress and heartache for myself. Because I had gone rigid where pain was concerned, I was also resistant to *God's* move in my life.

Pain is a tremendous motivator and, believe it or not, sometimes it is the only recourse God has to incentivize us to change our ways. Humanity enjoys comfort. If we could live forever in a cushioned, comfy bubble we would—we like a "*womb with a view*." This comfort we seek can be toxic and slowly killing us, but if it alleviates our pain, we will gravitate toward it anyway.

Pain is not the enemy! I know many people currently in very painful situations, and each will have the opportunity to associate their pain with blessing and deliverance. I also know many who have refused their pain and so missed the door to freedom. Too often we try to escape the pain only to find that it is increased instead.

When we refuse to accept pain as part of life, we can come to view it as abuse. We think that because God allows pain, He is abusing us. This is a dangerous train of thought. Do you react to the presence of pain by *accusing* the Source of life? A coyote will chew off his own foot to escape pain and capture, but we are not animals. As children of God, bowing is more conducive to Life than fight-or-flight.

The presence of pain does not always signal that something is wrong. Pruning the dead wood of the flesh can be quick and surgical, but painless? No. And too often, we find ourselves running around the operating table, screaming and avoiding the knife, while a gangrenous limb drags behind us.

I am not advocating masochism, but to believe in the delusion that life can be free of pain is foolhardy. Any course change brings pain, even when I am being increased. Sure, if I have been rooting around in the dirt of the flesh, my repentance and consequences are painful. But expanse and blessing can also bring the pain of change. Pain is inevitable because we're alive.

For our fathers used to correct us according to their own ideas during the brief days of childhood. But God corrects us all our days for our own benefit, to teach us His holiness. Now obviously no "chastening" seems pleasant at the time: it is in fact **most** *unpleasant [painful]! Yet when it is all over we can see that is has quietly produced the fruit of real goodness in the characters of those who have accepted it in the right spirit. So take a fresh grip on life and brace your trembling limbs. Don't wander away from the path but forge steadily onward. On the right path the limping foot recovers strength and does not collapse.*

Hebrews 12:10-13 PHILLIPS

Saying Yes to the Pain

If Christ is the Divine Yes and Amen, then my **every yes *to* Him is a yes *for* Him.**

For as many as are the promises of God, they all find their Yes [answer] in Him [Christ]. For this reason we also utter the Amen (so be it) to God through Him [in His Person and by His agency] to the glory of God.
2 Corinthians 1:20 AMP

Over the years, God has shown me the purpose behind certain suffering in my life, but understanding what God takes us through does not have power in and of itself. The power is in my yes to God and all He has done.

My yes is surrender to Him *as God*!

I do not minimize the pain being dealt with by some of us. Years of emotional abuse by a spouse, parental abandonment, hurtful scorn and mockery from siblings…all awful situations, I know. Each one is painful, but made even *more so* by resistance to the experience. Resistance is an active NO to God. And that NO marks the soul in negative ways.

I once knew a man who was relentlessly abused by his father. His father was an alcoholic and took out his pain on his son. Nothing this man did as a child was good enough for his father, who beat him mercilessly for every so-called failure.

This scenario is tragic and horrible, but how this man responded to his father's abuse is just as tragic: He was bitter and filled with hate. Now, I cannot say that anyone without Christ would do differently, but the boy's bitterness grew over the years into a man's insanity.

This man literally went insane and was committed to an asylum. And in that asylum, he met God.

God told him clearly that he had been turned over to the tormentors and he would have to forgive his father to be free. For months the Holy Spirit led him through the jungle of his bitter heart into the clearing of forgiveness and freedom. Shortly after he completed this great spiritual work, he was released from the asylum with a clean bill of mental health.

Was it fair that a drunken father abused his own child so horribly? No! But God required forgiveness for this man's health and sanity. And that work of forgiveness set him free of the prison of bitterness. This man is now healthy and has a powerful testimony of the need to forgive regardless of the offense. The Lord is using his tragedy to set many other captives free.

When we turn and look back at these kinds of situations, we have the choice to be bitter or liberated. Liberty is found in saying yes to God. YES to the pain God allowed, or even directed, for the purpose of our forming.

Recently the Lord asked me to say yes to a painful situation in my own life. I had to say yes to the whole thing with no caveats. No explanation was given for the pain, no excuse, and no defense—God owes me no justification for anything He allows or directs in my life. In this case, He just asked me to choose. So in tears, I said YES.

Why in the world would I say yes to God for painful events, seasons or even a lifetime of heartache? Because my yes has the power to pull out the poisonous stinger of pain. It is my surrender to the Great I AM, who makes one vessel for honor and another for dishonor. *God is sovereign*, and our yielding makes His presence and reality powerfully evident.

Saying YES to the pain in our lives is also the only way to take possession of the benefits. God showed me that when I resist accepting a situation, I also block the benefits I have earned by living through it. Pain in our lives is not pain for pain's sake. God is not a sadist! We are built for reward and motivated by return on investment. To say YES to the whole of my life is to reap all the rewards and benefits from my painful experiences. This is how we receive all the GOOD that God has planned for us!

And we know that God causes all things to work together for good to those who love God, to those who are called according to His purpose. For those whom He foreknew, He also predestined to become conformed to the image of His Son…
Romans 8:28-29 NASB

Pain is Simply Proof of Life

If I am in pain, does it mean I am resisting God? No. Just because you experience pain over a situation in life does not mean that you are resisting God's sovereignty. There is a difference between pain and torment. Torment is the direct result of my resistance to God, whereas pain is simply proof that I am alive. Pain is inevitable. If I am living life, I will experience pain. Torment, on the other hand, is evidence that I am in opposition to God.

If I am avoiding pain, I will also avoid Christ's Life. Life is the full color palette of emotions—joy, sadness, love, hate, pain and ecstasy. There is pain in growth, with change, while dying to something, even in loving others. Pain is part of our life experience.

In actuality, pain may be proof that I am in my process with God. Madam Guyon said, **"Every problem in life is from resistance to God. There is no problem that is not resistance to God."** What a confirmation! This is the statement of a person who has embraced the cross and accepted the pain of dying.

In her booklet, *The Great Lie*, Martha Kilpatrick says, *"If our response is not surrender to His will, it is rebellion."* This is the explanation for why resistance to God produces torment. It is because resistance is rebellion, and torment is the due consequence of rebellion. The torrent of agony is real *and just*. If we rebel against God, then we reap torment. I know this has been the case every time I have pushed back against God's Will, or at His Life being my life. I have felt the fires of hell licking my back.

Pain and suffering is part of life, while resistance is avoiding Life, which leads to torment. The enemy wants to convince us that pain is evil, that pain is punishment, that pain IS torment. But life reveals that pain is part of the cosmic quotient fashioned by God. Why else would hunger, desire, or passion hurt and cause pain? Pain is not the enemy.

The blessing of pain is that it will push us to utter dependence on Christ's Life. All of life is an invitation to see God perform His Will to His satisfaction. Pain is just a huge reminder that we need Him.

And Saul said, Who are You, Lord? And He said, I am Jesus, Whom you are persecuting. It is dangerous and it will turn out badly for you to keep kicking against the goad [to offer vain and perilous **resistance**].

Acts 9:5 AMP

Accept the Life God has Given

There is an ultimate YES required of each of us: ***Yes to ME!*** YES to my story's failures, flaws, and frailty. Just YES!

Does God not know the fallibility of my being? Does He not know that I am human? Of course, He is the Author of my story. This is not an excuse for sin, like, "Okay then, I was an absentee father and emotionally abusive. Deal with it because that is your story!" No, it is only after I have repented that I can say *YES* to my story and accept it. We all have to say yes to our story; it is the door to enter Christ's victory as well as His Life. Our YES is a surrender to His Lordship, His sovereignty, His God-ness.

God said to me, "Say yes to the mockery, the scorn, the abandonment and rejection—all the pains of your life." And when I did, my yes put it all back in His hands to deal with as He – my God! – saw fit. My YES yielded to Him and His choices as Master of my destiny. God is the Great I AM of my life. And my YES is my bowing worship of Him as God.

Now, what I have come to realize is that only **ONE** has the power to accept the life God has given me. Only His Son's Life, *Christ's very Life*, will ever say yes to the whole of my story. The unsaved man has no ability to embrace his life. Acquiesce to it, maybe, but receive it? Not so much. Only the born-again believer has the ability to make a YES transaction with the Father's choices for their life. The Father's choices are only embraced by His Son's Life. As I am *in Christ*, His Life becomes my acceptance of His own choices for me. Jesus is my YES to the Father.

For we are God's masterpiece. He has created us anew in Christ Jesus, so we can do the good things he planned for us long ago.
Ephesians 2:10 NLT

Yes, the Weight is Off of Me in The Great Exchange!

Faith concerns itself not with questions but with a person, and that person is JESUS.

Michael Wells
(Founder of Abiding Life Ministries, 1952-2011)

The secret of the Christian life is not that it is a changed life but an exchanged Life. Exchanging our old for His NEW.

Dr. O.S. Hawkins
(Author, pastor, Christian Businessman and Financial officer)

Living in the Rest of God

For we who have believed do enter that rest…
Hebrews 4:3 NKJV

Before we dig in to what it means to "enter that rest," let's establish what rest is—and is NOT. Is rest the same thing as leisure? Leisure has always been a word I associate with luxury and abundance. It conjures a vision of retirement and ease, like sailing a yacht into the sunset to enjoy my golden years. So I asked the Lord one day, "What is the difference between leisure and rest?" He immediately replied, "Effort!" What a strange reply! How in the world could leisure be *effort*?

Our Creator's call has always been to Rest and not to leisure. The Jewish Sabbath was a shadow of the intended reality—living in utter dependence continually on the Life of Christ. Rest is surrendering to the Life of Christ. I can be fully active and be *in* Rest. Rest is Christ's very Life. Rest is *Sabbath*.

Leisure is in total opposition to rest. While leisure may look like inactivity, in reality it is an active rebellion against the Life flow of Christ. Leisure is the effort to resist Christ's Life. It is relinquishment, a resignation *from* Life.

Christ is often very still in us. He *does* lead us to green pastures and lays us down beside still waters. What He does not do is give us liberty from His Life without penalty.

Dwelling in Rest is the choice to live continually dependent on Christ's Life to perform yours. It is eternal! Leisure is a selfish choice to retire from responsibility, and spirals downward into death. Leisure is as temporal as this present moment and only serves ME.

But the real tragedy of a life of leisure is that it will miss out on the adventure of Christ's Life lived in and through us.

Working on the Sabbath

How serious is God's call to honor the Sabbath Rest? The Book of Numbers speaks of a man who was caught gathering sticks on the Sabbath (Num. 15:32-36). This man was taken to Moses for judgment, and the Lord had him put to death by stoning at the hands of the assembly. This might seem extreme, but the moral of the story is that the Lord's holiness is far more important than getting our work done.

I am very fortunate not to have lived in those times, for I surely would have been stoned. I have often gathered my wood, hay, and stubble rather than *living* in the Sabbath rest. And all of my work is to be done out of a place of **rest** (from the Life of Christ) or it is a violation of the Sabbath.

This man with his bundle of sticks is a clear example of who we are without the life of Christ. We are all called to enter the rest. Hebrews says, *"Therefore, since a promise remains of entering His rest, let us* **fear** *lest any of you seem to have come short of it"* (Hebrews 4:1 NKJV). We are not to *perform* any work; we are only to live in Sabbath rest.

This stick bundler may have been a man who simply lost his perspective. The pressure of his responsibilities may have overtaken his fear of God. But God deemed this worthy of death. The stick bundler died that day. It would be hard for me to begin casting stones at him because I know that I, too, have put responsibility (getting the job done) above the Sabbath (the Life of Christ). I have valued my work and efforts over His Life and the rest I must fear not entering.

In the Old Testament, the rest was to be on the seventh day. No work was to be performed on that day. They were to rest from their labors just as God rested from His on the seventh day of Creation. The Sabbath was required to train and teach Israel how to live. They were slaves; all they knew was work. God knew we were not made for only work and without rest we would run ourselves into the ground. Rest is HOLY!

Then Christ came to up the ante, as He always did. For example, *"You have heard that it was said, 'Do not commit adultery.' But I tell you that anyone who* ***looks****..."* Jesus increased the requirement on everything because He became the solution to it ALL.

The Lord said you are a nation of priests, a holy nation and He fulfilled the Law of the Sabbath rest and so could say, come unto Me, I am your Rest (1 Peter 2:9). Christ's own Life is now our Sabbath rest. He performs, we rest. Our work and effort is but wood, hay and stubble, while His Life is eternal and transcendent. We are called to the Sabbath as a lifestyle. Christ's Life as my life is *His Life* in my life, and that's not my life as His life, it's HIM.

The message I take from this harrowing story in Numbers is that our work is death. We may no longer be stoned for failing to enter the Sabbath rest, and we might not even see the immediate consequences of living independently of Jesus, but if Christ's Life is not my life, I will be sowing to the wind regardless of what I get done. Who cares if I can build the world?! If it is not Christ's very own Life, it is temporal and ultimately death.

Let us therefore be diligent to enter that rest, lest anyone fall according to the same example of disobedience.
Hebrews 4:11 NKJV

Trying Hard to Abide

Having grasped how important Sabbath Rest was, years ago, I embarked on a journey to ABIDE! John 15:5 says, *"I am the vine, you are the branches; He who abides in Me and I in Him, he shall bear much fruit, for apart from Me you can do nothing."*

So I *tried* to abide. I attempted to work it out through quiet times. "Early mornings are the best," *I was told.* So I tried to remain in rest. I felt like I could struggle or strain my way into abiding. If I could just capture the Rest in a moment, maybe I could keep it going for life! Perhaps if I remained still enough, quiet enough, then I could and would abide. That did not happen.

What did I learn from the years of *TRYING to abide*? Abiding is Christ. Abiding is not found in a manufactured moment but in a life surrendered and yielded to the Lord. You abide by His abiding in you. You abide because your moments are held in His hands. My passionate desire to abide is actually HIS own desire for me to experience the intimacy of His Life. His heart swells as I desire to touch Him, for all desire comes from Him first. But my fleshly attempts to abide fail every time.

It is not during special moments that abiding is found, or even in my quiet times. Abiding is *Life*. Everywhere I walk, I abide because I am in Him. I am His dwelling, but first and foremost, He is *my* dwelling. *That* is abiding!

Working for a Quiet Time

Essential to abiding in Christ is genuine relationship with Him. And time is required to build a relationship with anyone, let alone Jesus Christ. So I spend time with Him to get to know Him, to value Him above myself, and to love Him. This is the essence of my quiet time. But what does that look like?

Do you approach your quiet time like a job? Are you going to work? Do you look to achieve a task? I have caught myself more than once *tackling* my time with the Lord rather than settling into it. I would function like I had a job to do, and come hell or high water, I *was* going to get it done.

One day I sat down and said to the Lord, "This is about You. I'm not on stage and I don't have to perform. No, I am here for You." Then I sat and waited. I was there for His pleasure. And what I discovered then is that the pressure to produce was gone.

This is not some magnanimous gesture on my part. I *need* this quiet time so much. I need my life's focus to be Jesus. I need to know that He is where all my days begin and end. I need to prefer Him to myself. But as far as the performance of a quiet time goes, He is the director. He is the guide; I just present myself. "Here is my life, my time, my heart (with all that entails). Here am I for You, Lord."

Occasionally I come to God as a servant rather than son. I look at it as if I am the one with all the needs, seeking the One with all the provision. Oh, that is so wrong. When I position my heart in this way, no wonder I come to get a task done. I have a shopping list that has to be filled by the Great Grocer and my payment is whatever gyrations He requires. Three worship songs, two chapters of scripture reading, thanking Him for what I got yesterday, a possible tear or two and then I get my order, right? Not for the son! A son comes to the Father with everything because all things are his. He comes to be with the Father out of love, not duty. A servant looks *to get* and a son looks *to be*. This removes all the pressure off the function of a quiet time and places all the focus on the Father.

If I am sitting with my Father as a son and stillness and silence is the result, then that is what He wants. If worship, reading, confession, or supplication happens, then it must be by His leading. I am not here to perform; I am here for His will.

I am a son, not a servant. I seek my Abba, not my eternal employer.

Arrested by Rest

Over the years, I diligently sought the Lord's abiding presence in order to enter into fellowship with God, but what *found me* was **Rest**. Life is about relationship. Isolating single attributes of the spiritual walk is not relational nor is it the actual Life. You might have the form but unless there is Christ, you have nothing but a facsimile.

They will act religious, but they will reject the ***power*** *that could make them godly.*
2 Timothy 3:5 NLT

I can amass all the habits of a spiritual life but without the *Source* of Life, I will be left with only behavior. I was seeking elements of the life, thinking it would bring me to Jesus, but no, **Life** had to come and get me. Jesus had to come and show me what abiding meant.

We do not *create* abiding; abiding is the Lord.
We do not *perform* rest; rest is Christ.
We do not *get* peace; peace is Jesus.

Let us therefore give diligence to enter into that rest, that no man fall after the same example of disobedience.
Hebrews 4:11 ASV

When the Bible says, "Enter into the rest," I am not entering a place, but Christ Himself. Rest is not a response to life I develop, but a faith I believe. I always thought rest was an obedience I had to achieve, but it is not. Rest is entering HIS LIFE. Only Christ's Life rests.

The true characteristics of a godly life are found in the Life itself, not outside of it. We cannot dictate abiding, we get into Him who is abiding. We cannot possess peace; we get into Him who is Peace.

We cannot attain rest; we get into Him who is Rest. And more importantly, He gets into us.

God used my goal of learning how to abide to lead me to the One *who is abiding*. The journey was not in vain. God used it as a tremendous motivator and defeating agent to guide me. My wandering in the wilderness of exertion led to exhaustion and my need of a power outside of myself.

Christ's Life in our new creation is the only hope of Godliness. All the fruits of the Spirit are the Life of Christ. We do not have to climb an awful Mt. Everest of human effort to obtain what is ours through faith.

Rest is neither something you get nor something you possess. **Rest is Christ.** And a "quiet time" is not about making things still and silent in an effort to abide; it is simply entering Christ's Life.

Struggling to Get Where I Already Am

Perhaps the very heart of entering the Sabbath Rest is *believing* that I am *in rest*. What is it in the psyche that attempts to convince the born-again believer that we're separated from God? Each morning I am tempted to believe that I come to Him, as if I have to *get* to Him. It is as though I was covered with a veil of doubt while I slept, and I must fight to remove it in order to start my day new with the Lord. Now, I speak as a son, born from above, not as someone still searching. I am saved. I evidence the new birth with a new life. Why then do I struggle to come in line with who I already am?

I found the answer to that question in Oswald Chambers' devotional, *My Utmost for His Highest*. In the May 28 devotion, Oswald discusses the day when you ask no further questions because you and the Father are one. So, I am *already* with the Father. I do not need to try so hard to *get* to Him, so when I do struggle, it is simply an issue of faith.

There is an assault on my faith to convince me that I am not where I am. The enemy's game is to skew the reality of the truth. Each morning I should come as one "there," not as one "arriving." Positionally, *I am in Christ*! So why is there a work to get where I already am?

We are destroying speculations and every lofty thing raised up against the knowledge of God, and we are taking every thought captive to the obedience of Christ…
2 Corinthians 10:5 NASB

The work is to demolish every argument and every pretense that sets itself up against the knowledge of God. I have work because I have an enemy, and my mind is so easily diverted. It is a worthy fight of faith, but the fight is not to *enter* the reality; my fight is silencing the *unreality*.

When I sit down to be with God, I am already in Christ with the Father (Ephesians 2:6). When I still myself to commune with the Lord, I am shedding the temporal to acknowledge the actual. What a crafty trick of the enemy—make us work to achieve what has already been given. Boy, this messes with the mind!

The mental work to *arrive* is counterproductive and a departure from the truth. You can't travel to where you already are, and to put forth the effort is not just a waste of time; *it is unbelief*.

Whenever I feel the schism, I can tear down that veil of delusion standing opposed to me. It is like being on a movie lot where there is a façade of a 1920s cityscape. It looks like I am in a city, but in actuality, I am on a movie lot. I can walk off the set at any time. And just as easily, I have the power and responsibility to cast down this unbelief.

The reality is that **you are** in Christ, seated with Him in the heavenlies. The enemy would have you believe that you are alone and pleading with the Father for His love and attention. Pshaw!

I choose to **believe** what actually IS: I am in Christ, in the Rest, and I have continual fellowship as we are ONE.

May they all be one, as You, Father, are in Me and I am in You. May they also be one in Us, so the world may believe You sent Me.
John 17:21 HCSB

What is the Work to Experiencing The Great Exchange?

The flesh-life (the self-life) and the Christ-life are continually at war with each other. Thus any attempt to live the abundant life in this world means spiritual warfare.

Edward F. Murphy
(Author on War and Warfare 1921-)

Choosing How to Think

Most, if not all, of our choices are born of how we see ourselves. We live our lives as a projection of how we see ourselves. My life is a billboard to the world of who I think I am. Like the emperor with no clothes, we walk about thinking we are covered, but all the while the world is witness to our inward parts.

Most of my poor choices over the years reflected how I viewed myself. I judged myself by old concepts and values and then made choices reflecting the old man rather than my new man in Christ. This is the hope of Satan. How he longs to capture us to the thinking of our old man rather than the new creation with a new nature!

Though God's grace is amazingly present this side of the cross, I still do not want to be passed over for my heavenly position because I am maintaining the wrong view of myself. The new creation is a New Man altogether. I have been saved from the old nature into a totally new reality. It is foolishness to continue to think and choose from that old life. My new creation is NOT constrained by the old nature and my divine destiny is God's promotion.

> *This means that our knowledge of men can no longer be based on their outward lives (indeed, even though we knew Christ as a man we do not know Him like that any longer). For if a man is in Christ he becomes a new person altogether—the past is finished and gone, everything has become fresh and new. All this is God's doing, for He has reconciled us to Himself through Jesus Christ; and He has made us agents of the reconciliation.*
>
> 2 Corinthians 5:16-18 PHILLIPS

Embracing My Cross Life

But realize this, that in the last days difficult times will come. For men will be lovers of self, lovers of money, boastful, arrogant, revilers, disobedient to parents, ungrateful, unholy, unloving, irreconcilable, malicious gossips, without self-control, brutal, haters of good, treacherous, reckless, conceited, lovers of pleasure rather than lovers of God, ***holding to a form of godliness, although they have denied its power****; avoid such men as these.*
2 Timothy 3:1-5 NASB (emphasis mine)

This passage speaks of those who live a religious life without the exchanged Life. Without going to our personal cross with Christ, we have no exchange of life with Him. The cross is where we surrender our life to death, making the transaction. We cannot have that exchange bar going to the cross. We cannot be free from our old Adamic life unless we go to the cross with Christ. The legal transaction is performed *only* on the cross.

I have attempted to surrender while avoiding death. I thought the surrender was the death, but there is a surrender that effects *no* immediate change. It is the surrender that is made in choice only. A choice? How can you really choose to bow but not die? I have!

Peter made a *choice*, saying, "Even if I must die with You," but the cross-life had not yet hit the Peter-life. Peter stated his intention and this was heard by the Lord. The intention of his heart would eventually be made reality, but God could only perform this after the Peter-life died. The good news is that God hears the intention of our hearts and will bring us through to the other side of performance.

I cannot have Christ's life without losing mine.

I believed that a bowed will was what the Lord required – a submitted self to the process. Yet I got up after each surrender and lived. How could I do this? Simply. If we believe in our old life and see it as a yielded entity without the actual death that is performed on the cross, we are deceiving ourselves. But if this choice to die is truly made, then God hears it and He is committed to take you to the next step, which is to embrace the cross and lose your own life.

Seeking His Kingdom Not Mine

But seek first HIS kingdom and HIS righteousness, and ***ALL*** *these things will be given to you as well.*
Matthew 6:33 NIV

Seeking first the kingdom and Christ's righteousness is no less a choice than embracing the cross. Everything we need to live this life comes by seeking HIS kingdom and HIS righteousness. Not everything *I WANT* but certainly everything **I need**! And for those of us who have occasionally seen God as a miser, our need is not just the minimal requirements to scrape by in life. Our Father is an abundant supplier, a Supplier beyond **ALL** that we could ask or think. For the man or woman who seeks Jesus' kingdom and righteousness, everything needed to live a kingdom lifestyle will be provided.

However, in a world that seeks personal fulfillment and instant gratification, this is harder to do than it would seem. Seeking is a choice. To seek HIS kingdom and HIS righteousness is the denial of SELF. This seeking is done by being His disciple. And to be a disciple, the Amplified Bible says we must "disown self, forget, lose sight of self and our own interests, refuse and give up completely our self."

Many people attempt to walk a righteous path. I have sought to BE righteous through seemingly righteous acts, but this inevitably ends in failure. I have witnessed others building their own kingdoms, just as I have sought to build mine, hoping for the "God-housekeeping" seal of approval. Yet all my righteous deeds and acts of kingdom building have been farces and fairytales. To seek HIS kingdom and HIS righteousness is to seek His very own LIFE. In His Life is true Life, while in self-pursuit, I cannot find life at all.

Worry can plague us, day in and day out. Our doubts can ride us, convincing us that we will not have what we need to live. And I believe this is not just material supply. It is not just clothing, shelter, and food; it is the supply of everything needed for relationship with God – hunger for God, desire for holiness, and purity of thought. The promise of God in Matthew is that if we will but seek His kingdom and His righteousness, which is found in His Life, we will have everything for life *and* godliness. The key to this promise and all other promises is Christ Himself.

He has by His own action given us everything that is necessary for living the truly good life, in allowing us to know the one who has called us to Him, through His own glorious goodness. It is through Him that God's greatest and most precious promises have become available to us men, making it possible for you to escape the inevitable disintegration that lust produces in the world and to share in God's essential nature.
2 Peter 1:3-4 Phillips

Where Does Righteousness Come From?

I dug into scriptural promises earlier in "It IS About Me," but I have a specific revelation to touch on here as well. This particular promise in the scripture is about righteousness. Some of David's references to "my righteousness" in the Psalms make me wince. Psalm 18, for instance, where several times David says, *"Reward me and repay me **according** to my righteousness."* My reaction is, "According to MY righteousness? Yikes, then I am in trouble! I do not feel righteous at all!" If I get what I deserve or am due according to *my righteousness,* I am not going to be doing too well.

My vision of righteousness is limited and erratic. "Oh, today I am doing really well!" "Oops, I just screamed at the lady who cut me off while driving…" The righteousness *I produce* is very subjective. So, if God gives to me based on "my righteousness," then my supply will be very sporadic and limited, too.

*The Lord rewarded me according to **my righteousness**; He repaid me according to the cleanness of my hands. For I have kept the ways of the Lord and have not turned from my God to wickedness. Indeed, I have kept all His ordinances in mind and have not disregarded His statutes. I was blameless toward Him and kept myself from sinning. So the Lord repaid me according to **my righteousness**, according to the cleanness of my hands in His sight.*
Psalms 18:20-24 HCSB

I stared at this with the Lord and this DOES relate to me and you. Our righteousness comes from Another. Righteousness comes from the Life of the Lord Jesus. My righteousness is established in Him because *I am no more.* It is no longer I but HE (Gal. 2:20). My life is in the heavens and now the righteousness I have is His very Life. Oh, this changes everything.

You might say, "Well duh, John!" But this solved a dilemma I had in reading these scriptures. From the time I was a young Christian, I had felt condemned by these scriptures. I thought to myself, "But God, I do not *feel* righteous. Maybe I can be someday." And this train of thought left me lacking and wanting. It actually separated me from God, which was not the point at all.

My righteousness has nothing to do with *my efforts*, but only my faith. Christ is righteousness and He is my life. These scriptures are encouraging to me now. I join David in saying, "Lord, reward me according to my righteousness" (which is HIS Life).

Christ came to increase the requirements on our lives. Jesus said, *"You have heard that it was said, An eye for an eye and a tooth for a tooth. But I tell you, don't resist an evildoer. On the contrary, if anyone slaps you on your right cheek, turn the other to him also."* He upped the ante to make it utterly impossible to live according to "my righteousness." This life requires Christ's righteousness, His strength, His reward, and His very Person.

We will be judged according to our hearts, not just our actions. And which one of us has not had a covetous thought? Who among us has not had jealousy, murder, adultery, and deceit in our hearts? We are all sinners. And Jesus died to save us all, exchanging our sinful lives for His righteous one.

Jesus lives His righteousness in you, making it your righteousness. Hallelujah! We are rewarded for the Life of the Rewarder. We are repaid for the efforts of our Redeemer. Psalm 18 does not isolate us from God but instead displays His intent and performance. Christ is your righteousness and because He is righteous, *so are you.*

Doing The Work of Decision

There is a daily work of deciding that is simply part of being alive, but it is more powerful than we know. To turn a life around, we choose a new direction, and then follow through with our momentary and daily choices. It is like the navigation of a ship. We change the trajectory of our lives by setting a new course. With this new destination in mind, we navigate the course with our daily choices.

Many Christians want to believe that a choice is a *once and for always* thing. Who wouldn't? Deciding and choosing is hard work. But the one-time choice does not tend to be long lasting. Once I set my will with my course, then it must be supported with gradual rudder adjustments to keep me on that course. This is the WORK of decision.

When navigating a large sailing vessel, the captain plots out a course, which sets the direction. He maintains that direction every moment along the journey. And if that vessel sails off course, it might take time to course-correct. Impatience and frustration does nothing to assist in this process. The captain can fume and rant all day long, but that is simply exhausting the energy he needs to make an actual change. In the same way, changing the direction of my life is not helped by frustration. In fact, frustration can thwart my efforts to change.

Despair can certainly fuel your decisions, but depression only zaps the energy you need to live out that choice. I know this one well. It is easy to sink into depression rather than doing the work of choosing.

I have witnessed people drastically changing the direction of their whole lives. And in the day-to-day living, it was almost imperceptible. But after a season, that choice becomes clear. They had righted their vessel and were sailing firmly on a new course. The internal work of decision was manifested for all to see. It was beautiful!

Consider well and watch carefully the path of your feet, and all your ways will be steadfast and sure.
Proverbs 4:26 AMP

Resolving to Live as a New Creation

When talking about the Great Exchange, certain questions tend to be asked. One of them centers on free will and salvation: Did the "Old Man" die once and for all at the Cross, and if so, does not that mean Romans 7 is just a phase to go through and leave behind? This question is essential to understanding the exchanged Life.

The core of the exchanged Life is, "Christ's life as my life is **His** life *in* my life." Most of us, if honest, struggle with this. "If I am dead, then why do I seem so alive? And the more I learn about His Life as my life, the less I feel I am able to do it." There is the rub!

Some exchanged life believers think that once we receive the revelation that we died with Christ on the cross, it is all Christ's life in us going forward. They think that we no longer have to struggle with moment-by-moment choices because everything is now Christ. This would be GREAT—*if true*! But though there is a once and for all choice in salvation, this does not mean that from then on, everything we do is Christ. I cannot ***acknowledge*** the truth and ***resolve*** to live as the new creation. To resolve to live the new man is effort and determination, both of which are characteristics of the old man. That does not work. Though the truth sets me free, I am not freed from responsibility simply because I know the truth. Here is why.

I believe with all my heart that God wants union with us as His Bride. He yearns for our fellowship and interaction, but that is experienced in our utter dependence on Him. By simply acknowledging and resolving, I am seizing a new kind of independence from God; as if having the *truth* means I no longer need Him. If I were able to make a single choice and then be free from further choices, it would defeat the purpose of this life. This life is for relationship, as well as training to reign and rule with Christ. I am trained to reign with Christ by daily taking up my cross! And what is that cross? Choosing between God's Will or my own.

Christ's Life as my life does not alleviate me from choosing God's Will and being dependent on Him. The finished work of the cross frees me to make this choice and live it out. The cross did not win me independence from God; it unified me to His LIFE.

Then He said to them all, "If anyone desires to come after Me, let him deny himself, and take up his cross daily, and follow Me."
Luke 9:23 NKJV

Unlocking Victorious Christianity

The work of choosing does not just embrace the cross, it also unleashes Resurrection Life. But how? In Martha Kilpatrick's audio series *The Way,* she makes this statement: "All the requirements of the New Covenant are on the Life of Christ." Such good news! The New Covenant is Christ's Life satisfying the Father's requirements, but I actively participate with my choices. My decision for Christ's Life to be my life is not optional. And our lives clearly show what we have chosen.

Now, righting a life takes time. You do not turn an aircraft carrier on a dime. It takes miles and miles to reverse that course. And after a lifetime of choosing one direction, it may take time to establish another course.

The Word says, "What a man **sows**, he will reap." Unfortunately, this is usually referred to in a negative light: "Hey, if you do bad, bad will result!" But this *also* applies to our godly choices. Obvious I know, but hopeful, yes? If I sow the seeds of God-choices, He will assure my reaping of His Life. God is not mocked: I get what I choose in life, both the bad and *good*.

Jesus said to sinners, "Go and sin no more!" How could He set them an impossible task *unless* it was actually possible? "Do the work of choosing!" He gave us His Spirit to direct our choices and the power of His Life so that we could succeed. If I am not happy with my direction, I have the power of decision to navigate another course. This is true even when it looks impossible. Is God so cruel as to allow only the negative effects of His Word? No! If I sow choices *for* Him, will He not reap from those choices? Yes!

Though Satan tempts me to believe my choices have no power, I have been given the power to choose by God Himself. It is not only my *right* but my *responsibility*. And if anything hinders the performance of my choice, God is able to remove it.

I am responsible for the direction of my life, while Christ's Life is the *performance* of it. This IS the New Covenant.

The heart of man plans his way, but the Lord establishes his steps.
Proverbs 16:9 ESV

From *The Mystery of the Gospel* CD series by Martha Kilpatrick:

> "Norman Grubb said, 'All of the commands of the New Testament are to Christ **in you**.' This takes the entire burden off of you. All you have to do, and the only thing you can do, is to *present your body*.
>
> "When I first stepped into this I had a stack of mail on my desk. I couldn't answer them; I'm just not good at answering letters. But I said, 'Lord, You have some letters on Your desk, and when You're ready to answer Your mail, *my body is available*.' And in the easiest way it was done in a week.
>
> "Jesus is the fulfillment of my destiny and He is the fulfillment of yours. He *is* your role! He is your motherhood. He is your sisterhood, your daughterhood, your sonship, your role as a wife, and your role as a husband. He performs all these roles and He must be the one living them. *Success* is Jesus living your life.
>
> "There is only one Life in the universe that conquered the test of the wilderness. There's only one

> Life in whom God is pleased. And that Life can live in you every minute that you allow Him the privilege to do so.
>
> "In Romans 12:1, when it says *present your body*, I understand in the Greek that it is speaking of a one-time offering. And I think it's true that there is a *first* time offering of your body. But I have to be reminded constantly that this IS the solution to life—letting Him *do it*. This is the **mystery of the gospel**! You let Christ live in your life, in your body, and He will take you into His glory.
>
> "One day the Lord asked me to do something and I obeyed Him and then I was just in such bliss. I said, 'Oh Lord, I would just love to live here!' It was such joy and bliss, just like a cloud. And He said, 'You're not in your bliss, you're in Mine!' He had bliss and joy on this earth living in the Father – in the cloud. Jesus lived in the cloud! And when you will let Him BE, He will take you up into that glory. You *can* experience it in this life. Glory is a gift that He wants us to experience *in this life!*
>
> "...**The covenant is God doing it all *for* you and that's where the glory is.** Letting God do all for you. Letting Him be your character. Letting Him be your love. There is only one person in the universe who ever loved—that's Jesus! There is only one Person who ever pleased God—JESUS."

This *IS* the **mystery of the Gospel**! True, victorious Christianity is Jesus living your life, not you—His own Life, His own will, His own character, His own purity, and His own love. Living continually in the cloud of His glory is to experience His very Life as your life. Imagine, not imitation, or effort, or goodness, or pretending. Living *constantly* in the cloud of His glory, in the beams of His smiling pleasure, is letting Him express His life through you.

Your job? Present your body to Jesus Christ for His Life-filling joy. This is your reasonable service and act of worship. Why reasonable? Because your efforts have never resulted in victorious Christianity. It is reasonable because if everything is provided for you, why would you try to break new trail? Yet I still have to be continually reminded. Don't you?

I beseech you therefore, brethren, by the mercies of God, that you present your bodies a living sacrifice, holy, acceptable to God, which is your reasonable service.
Romans 12:1 NKJV

The Way to
The Great Exchange

We think of the Christian life as a "changed life' but it is not that. What God offers us is an 'exchanged life,' a 'substituted life,' and Christ is our Substitute within.

Watchman Nee
(Chinese church leader, Christian teacher, Author, Martyr, 1903-1972)

The Benefit of Living in Christ

The mind of the flesh will never grasp the "*Christ in me*" reality; that is utter and complete foolishness to the mind of the flesh. Actually, it goes beyond foolishness. "Christ in me" is abhorrent to my flesh because it is not reliant on the self! It is an affront to everything we work so hard to achieve – to be victorious, spiritual, godly, and righteous. I am none of these, no matter how hard I try.

But people who aren't spiritual can't receive these truths from God's Spirit. It all sounds foolish to them and they can't understand it, for only those who are spiritual can understand what the Spirit means.
1 Corinthians 2:14 NLT

The benefits of living IN Christ are as multifaceted and personal as we are. Why? Because living IN Christ is Christ living as YOU, and this manifests uniquely and individually in each life. One may be a police officer, another a construction worker, yet another a mother and housewife, and still another a ruler or politician – all individuals with distinct lives and roles.

The benefit of living IN Christ is that **my life is done *for* me, *through* me.** I am **given** the victory! This is the only real victory we experience in our spiritual life. Christ, Himself, does what only He can do. Your spiritual life is not dependent on your performance. Your performance only prevents THE Life from manifesting.

In my early Christian days, I wanted to take part in the performance of this life. I wanted to give my best in service to the Lord. I wanted to make my Heavenly Father proud of ME. Yet I found instead that my service was detrimental to the Kingdom.

If I could *be* the life in me, then I would have something to offer to the King of Glory. I would have an offering to present to Him, something to make Him proud. And I would take great pride in that accomplishment. I would excitedly present my gift of life: "Aren't you proud of ME, Daddy?" **NO!** There is only one, *yes One*, Life that brings pleasure to the Father. Only One Life satisfies His requirements and only One Life makes Him proud—the Life of His SON, Jesus Christ!

For you are saved by grace through faith, and this is not from yourselves; it is God's gift—not from works, ***so that no one can boast.***
Ephesians 2:8-9 HCSB

God has chosen what is insignificant and despised in the world—what is viewed as nothing—to bring to nothing what is viewed as something, ***so that no one can boast*** *in His presence. But it is from Him that you are in Christ Jesus, who became God-given wisdom for us—our righteousness, sanctification, and redemption, in order that, as it is written:* ***The one who boasts must boast in the Lord.***
1 Corinthians 1:28-31 HCSB

The benefit of living IN Christ is that I get to experience the easy yoke and light burden. He chose those of us who are weak and foolish so it would be He in me and not ME. Life is done IN me, for me, as Christ Himself lives through me. My life stands for a victory I neither authored nor accomplished. I am a benefactor of the grace and choosing of my God. I have no badge of accomplishment or achievement.

I have been crucified with Christ and ***I no longer live, but Christ lives in me****. And the life that I now live in my body, I live by faith, indeed,* ***by the faithfulness of God's Son****, who loved me and gave Himself for me.*
Galatians 2:20 CEB

I do have a crown, which I will throw down at the feet of the One who earned it. My victory and life is Christ's triumph and success as He earned His Father's pleasure through me. I am a trophy of His glowing grace and ability to complete what He has started. Neither my talents nor giftings earn me a reward; they were merely instruments that the Son of God played to honor His own Father. I am the eternal benefactor of a Reward Jesus earned for Himself.

Christ's Life is My Life

We cannot have our flesh and our spiritual life, too. It is an either/or choice: Him or me. The *first* Adam and *last* Adam cannot cohabitate. We are literally taking the broad way of destruction by not living the exchanged life. But as long as we know which path we are walking, there should be no shock at the consequences.

Following Christ precludes giving CPR to my old life. There is a "do not resuscitate" tag on my corpse. That old man must die . . . *or not.* Again, it is a God-given RIGHT to make this choice. We are free to choose the flesh over God, but the reward of performing mouth-to-mouth on a long since dead person is at best, chapped lips and worst, ingestion of decay.

Provoked flesh shares a common refrain: "*What about MY fulfillment? What about MY dreams coming true?* Well, we can choose our dreams if we want. We can chase after them with all we have, but then the King of Glory will not be enthroned in us.

What were we saved for?
What were we saved from?
What were we saved to?

Our salvation was not for OUR fulfillment. "*But wait, I was told at the altar of my salvation that I would have life abundant!*" Yes, this is true, but it is not an abundance of YOU. It is His abundant Life, an abundance of *Christ's Life*. It will be His abundant fulfillment, His abundant joy, His abundant satisfaction. It is Jesus' glorified Life, His offering to the Father, and His reward. **HIM, not us!**

Will Christ be satisfied or will we? We can and will have satisfaction in Him, but it is His fulfillment first, not ours. This is counter to most everything I hear preached and hence, this could be the most unpopular words EVER written! But it is the reality nonetheless.

Do you think that because I am writing this I get a pass and my dreams remain intact? No, my original vision for my life has been crushed, annihilated, destroyed. All the years of seeking my own fulfillment were shipwrecked by saying "yes" to His Life in me. So am I left vanquished? NO! I am given TRUE, REAL LIFE. But it is not for me; it is for Jesus.

The Gospel is not FOR you. While you are the one who was saved, you were saved FOR Him. This is where the narrow way takes us. Not in finally getting that man/woman who will bring us unending happiness and fill that deep hole inside. Not in having our parent finally say they are proud of us after a lifetime of rejection. Not by having a ministry that will bring Him glory . . . oh, and me too! No, Christ gave His life so I could follow Him, and relinquishment of my life is what it means to follow Jesus – Him not me.

It is not grace to let someone think they are okay because they have now achieved some sort of soulish nirvana. I am not supposed to widen the berth to make people feel accepted and comfortable. Death is horrid, but that is what is required. Christ died that I might live, not my own life, but that I might live together with Him (see 1 Thessalonians 5:10).

> *I have been crucified with Christ; and it is no longer I who live, but Christ lives in me; and the life which I now live in the flesh I live by faith in the Son of God, who loved me and gave Himself up for me.*
> Galatians 2:20 NASB

Emulation of Christ? That is still me!
Guidance by Jesus? That's still me!

Following (as effort)? Still me!
Emergence? ME!

It is NO LONGER I who live but Christ lives in ME.

Then What's in it for ME?

Whether it is selling an item, conveying a thought, or inspiring to action, we are motivated by gain for self. Even God set us up with reward as a principle. So you might ask, "If this life is for Jesus, then what's in it for ME?"

Scripture says, *"I have been crucified with Christ; and it is* ***no longer*** *I who live, but Christ lives in me"* (Gal. 2:20). Essentially, you were born into a fallen world as a vessel of death. All your self-inspired good deeds are selfishly motivated, and even your 'human love' is faulty at best. Then Christ came for you and you were saved from this body of death by being crucified with Him. Your old nature was laid in the tomb WITH Christ. He joined you in eradicating your old man and ending all the death that erupted from your independent life. You could not pay your own penalty, so Jesus clothed Himself with your humanity and took you where you had to go—the grave. We have to die!

The first reward of salvation is FREEDOM from our slavery. No longer do we have to support this wayward life. We were liberated from the sting of death and living an empty life. We were given a once-and-for-all freedom. But, you have to come in line with the reality of the truth **that you are free**. Weirdly, it is about the *awareness* of this reality, not *achieving* the fact. It is finished; we just have to learn and walk out what was accomplished on the cross.

The second reward of "No longer I but Christ": abundant LIFE. Not only did Christ die your death and take you to the grave, but now He lives your life. *"How in the world does that work?"* When Christ rose from the grave and ascended into heaven, you went with Him. Your resurrected life is with Him, now. *"So how could this be good news, what about ME?"* Well, His beautiful Life can now live yours. *"But what about ME?!"* We are able to watch His glorious, fruit-filled Life live for the Father. And His joy is yours, because you are in Him. His satisfaction is yours, because you are in Him. His fulfillment is yours, because you are in Him.

See, what appears to be the loss of your life is a gaining of **ALL** Life. No, it is not your self-life, but we established that *that life* was simply futile and destructive. The life you lost was a torment, but the Life you gained is magnificent. Because it is no longer you who lives but Christ, His satisfaction is yours! You seek His fulfillment because you are one and this brings *you* complete fulfillment. You are not a paper doll of a person; no, you are full and intact, unique and individual. The expression of His life through your shell is unlike anyone else in the entire world—as unique and matchless as a fingerprint. But it is His Life in you. This is the mystery of Christ, your hope of glory.

It is not a logical, mentally attainable thing. This is a truth that requires surrender. You will not ever figure this out in your head, but you can experience its multifaceted actuality. You can say, "I am very much alive." This entire truth is a contradiction to the evidence that you see and feel. But its certainty is received by faith, a faith that pleases Him.

For you died to this life,
*and your real life is **hidden** with Christ in God.*
Colossians 3:3

Truly Living, Not I But Christ

"I have been crucified with Christ and I no longer live, but Christ lives in me" (Gal. 2:20). To the masses of my fellow wounded humans out there, this can seem like just another statement used to club us with rejection. But God is not saying, "NOT YOU, you're disgusting!" Oh, the enemy loves to twist a gift into another brick in the wall of rejection and disapproval. This is not the heart of God at all. "Not I but Christ" is not God looking for my complete eradication; He is inviting my *participation*. How can it be "He NOT me" yet invite my involvement?

Union! I can be no closer to Christ than to be in union, He in me and I in Him. Yes, the Source of my life must BE His, but the whole thing is set up so I might have complete participation. How? As a vessel, witness and observer!

I asked God for a simple picture of this—a simple, earthly picture for an extremely heavenly thing. How can you capture the mystery of God in a common object lesson? Not easily, for sure! But here is what God gave me: The exchanged life is like a man working in his garden, wearing gloves. I am the glove and Christ is the Life in the glove. It is His Life and identity in me.

God is not burdening His children with the responsibility to perform His dictated tasks. God does not send us to work alone in His garden for Him; we go into His garden and He works *through us.*

Christ's life as my life is His life *in* my life, and I witness it as the miracle it is. I know who I am on my own. I saw what my *self-life* produced. So now that I am His, free from my independent life, why would He send me back into the world to live independent from Him? He would not! That would be like giving a recovering alcoholic the job of taste-testing whiskey.

When at first I heard the scripture 'Not I but Christ,' my wounded self wept. I wanted to be a part of it all. If I were involved, maybe I could make God pleased with me. Somehow I could prove that my self-life was not the vilest thing in the whole world, that I was not a complete failure, and that I could manage to do something right. I read this Word through the lens of rejection and ascribed to God the worst motives. Nothing could be further from the truth. God set up the reality for me to witness His Life firsthand – a ringside seat. Can you see why the enemy would want to twist and thwart this reality?

It is a wonderful privilege to witness Jesus' very nature performed through you. He is the source of all Life. You get to watch His Life be lived in you, and you are ONE. You are not eradicated; you are included in the most intimate union possible.

Christ indwells you to express Himself *through you.*

He has granted to us His precious and magnificent promises,
so that by them you may become
partakers of the divine nature.
2 Peter 1:4 NASB

How Do I Let Christ Live My Life?

Here is the Holy Grail of all questions: "How do I let Christ live my life?" Though it should be lived out practically in every aspect of our lives, there is no 1-2-3 methodology to walking this out. There is no fixed set of rules to follow into union with Christ. The fruit of methods is animatronic death.

However, I do have some tips that I have gleaned along the way. First, "Not I but Christ" is a mystery. It is one of the most mysterious things in the universe. I believe the Word of God is filled from cover to cover about this great mystery. So, if it is a mystery, then it must be revealed by the Holy Spirit. I have to receive from God the revelation of "Not I but Christ." Wisdom Himself must give it to each of us. We ask, knock, even beg for it—and then wait for it to be given.

Now if 'Not I but Christ' is a mystery that must be grasped by revelation, then it also must be received by faith. Faith is the only thing that will accept something so otherworldly. And there is only one type of person that will release himself to the realm of the remarkable, and that is the little child.

Christ said, "I tell you the truth, anyone who doesn't receive the Kingdom of God **like a child** will never enter it" (Mark 10:15), and "Truly, I say to you, unless you turn and **become like children**, you will never enter the kingdom of heaven" (Matthew 18:3).

So *achieving* "Not I but Christ" or *mastering* this reality is impossible. But it is important enough to God that if you *abandon* yourself to receiving it, He will do the work of getting you there.

For it is God who is at work in you,
both to will and to work for His good pleasure.
Philippians 2:13 NASB

God is by no means attempting to frustrate us in this. It is not an unobtainable or just-out-of-our-reach reality. But it is impossible to *make* it happen. I won't study my way into it (I've got a stack of books if you want to borrow them.). I won't work my way into it (Anyone have a pumice stone? My calluses are rough!). I cannot speak the right mantra to make it a reality (I have a sore throat from trying anyway!). No, I am to let go and become a little child, with all my wonder and fascination, and Christ will bring forth His satisfaction and delight. His good pleasure is that we would know "the riches of the glory of this mystery, which is Christ in you, the hope of glory" (Colossians 1:27).

So Is the Church Failing?

I have heard it said many times that the church is failing. That she is laying down on the job and wrinkling her wedding dress. I have heard it said that the world is passing away in degradation, while we the church are fluffing the pillows in our pews. But I tell you, reader, this is *not* true.

The church is **not** failing the world! What we see all too often is the failure of those who *call* themselves the church. This is not a finger pointing session; I am not calling out any denomination or sect. I am shooting so much higher than earthly organizations. I am talking about a heavenly reality.

Who is the Church? Church is not a group organized under the name of Christ. It is not a gathering of people with a message. And it is not a building established for members to have a community and preach the gospel. **The Church is Christ!** Not *for* Christ, not *about* Christ and not even *with* Christ—***just*** *Christ.*

Don't let anyone condemn you... Their sinful minds have made them proud, and ***they are not connected to Christ, the head of the body****. For he holds the whole body together with its joints and ligaments, and it grows as God nourishes it.*
Colossians 2:18-19 NLT

What we tend to find out in the world might be *a* church, but it is not THE Church. The Church is not defined by an organization or a building; it is identified by the Life of Christ. It is either Christ or it is not THE Church. It might be a nice club, a community circle, or an outreach group for charity, but it is not Church. Again, *Church is Christ.*

So if Church is Christ, then the actual Church cannot be failing. Unless you are willing to say Christ is a failure, you cannot say that His Church is failing. How can I say this? Because Christ is Head of the Church and the Members of His Body are vessels of Christ's Life. The Word says this very clearly: "I have been crucified with Christ; and it is no longer I who live, but *Christ lives in me*" (Galatians 2:20). If I have died and my life is hidden with Christ in God, then it is *Christ not me* (Colossians 3:3). The great mystery of the ages is that I am not and *He is* (Colossians 1:26-27).

When you see Church, you are witnessing Christ. We are all one in His Body (Ephesians 3:6). Not like many people all under Christ, but **Christ Himself**. The *Church is Christ!*

The Church is Christ's Life, His Energy, His Purpose—*Him*. All else is just man's efforts *for Christ*, but that isn't the Church. Human effort is NOT Christ—so it is not Church. Church is Christ living His Life through His Body. Many have defined the members of the Body of Christ like we would define members in a service organization. But members of His Body are not just individuals with a similar focus, any more than the members of your own physical body. My body is me. My arm is not just gallantly trying to be unified with the rest of my body. *It is ME!* In the same way, Christ's Body is Christ.

As with everything in the Bible, reality is paradoxical. "I am here, so how can my life be Christ? How can my life be hidden in the heavenlies, when I am so apparently living? How can I be crucified with Christ and still walking, talking and living now?" Only by faith in the Son of God (Galatians 2:20).

Cain brought an offering but the offering was not accepted. God required blood not good intent. And this is true even today. God is looking for the acceptable Life of His Son, not my attempts to serve, please or placate.

The Church is not failing, because Christ is not failing. The question is not whether the Church is failing the world or not, *it is whether you are Church*. Are you living the Mystery of the Gospel? Is Christ your Life or are you just giving it a courageous effort?

Jesus paid a high price so that my living earthly expression would be Him and not me. He made the reality possible. Yes, it is mind-melting, but this great Mystery is the Gospel. God gave the Life of His Son and the Holy Spirit to perform His will in my body. I am the Body of Christ, and the Church is not failing. The Church is flourishing!

I am He, He is me, and we all are One Body.

What is the Will of God?

The Will of God for me is **Christ**. The absolute Will of God for John Enslow's life is "Christ in me." Not my achievements, not my fulfillment, not my legacy...but HIS!

My old self has been crucified with Christ. It is no longer I who live, but Christ lives in me. So I live in this earthly body by trusting in the Son of God, who loved me and gave Himself for me.
Galatians 2:20 NLT

Jesus Christ died and *He and I* were resurrected so that He could now *BE* my life. He did not die just so I could squeak by into heaven under grace. Nor was it a sacrificial death to mop up my mess so I could do it better. And He certainly was not crucified so that we could eternally hang out together. No, Jesus conquered death so He could *be* my life. Christ's death bought my ability to live in the absolute will of God.

I can live in the Will of God! Is it painless? No. Glorious? Yes! Christ in you *costs* you everything, and yet *gives* you Everything. Even in writing this book, I am bowing to the Will of God. I wanted to go to a special place with friends and family, yet here I sit because His Will for me is to stay home and write. And as I sit here, I keep thinking of other things I need to get done, but instead I am writing. And in the deep recesses of my heart, I admit to asking the question, "Is this really Your Will, Father?"

Sometimes the Will of God is readily apparent, and other times not as much. Christ's Life in my life is a work of surrender. It is the discipline of listening. It is the yielding of time.

Christ's Life is not in my performance but in my soul's prostration.

I can – and do! – contend for the Life of Christ as Christ in me. It is my heart to see in my life "He not I." But it requires great faith in His resurrected Life, utter vulnerability to Him as God, and a huge YES to Him that overshadows what I want for me. While *Christ in you* is satisfaction, glory, and eternal significance, this comes after a great big NO to myself.

Oswald Chambers says:

> "The one marvelous secret of a holy life lies not in imitating Jesus, but in letting the perfections of Jesus manifest themselves in my mortal flesh. Sanctification is 'Christ in you.' It is His wonderful life that is imparted to me in sanctification, and imparted by faith as a sovereign gift of God's grace. Am I willing for God to make sanctification as real in me as it is in His word?
>
> "...Sanctification is an impartation, not an imitation."

Therefore if any man [be] in Christ, [he is] a new creature: old things are passed away; behold, all things are become new.
2 Corinthians 5:17 KJV

There is One Thing in The Great Exchange

"I must be born anew. That is why Christ took me with Himself down into the grave and brought me forth a new creation."

F.J. Huegel
(WWI chaplain, missionary, prolific writer and well-traveled speaker, 1889-1971)

Can I Love God More?

Since the Garden of Eden, we all find it impossible to live this life. I have heard it described as "take a step and sin." In the Old Testament, we needed the blood of sheep and goats to atone for our sins, and a priest to mediate on our behalf. None were exempt from the blood sacrifice, not even the priests bearing the offering.

Then Christ came to be our atonement—the Bridge to span the gap we dug on our own. Our impossible task to love God was made possible with the Life of One who loves Him exclusively. Jesus became for us the Love we lacked, not in judgment or condemnation but as our only Solution.

I am not expected to BE the love He desires. I am only to *receive* the Life and Love He desires. I am a vessel only, built to contain this Life and Love. Any attempt on my part to manufacture life or love is a farce. I have no ability to produce, only to receive.

My human love is paltry and insufficient to satisfy the King of Glory. Though I have a high opinion of my love, it is pale and anemic compared to His. The best of my love is still selfish.

We are incapable of true, selfless love, so in steps Christ. He *is* the desire and the love God requires of us. And if I didn't have the Son's desire for His Father in me, I would never even think about Him, much less love Him. Am I alone in this? I think not! Christ's Love and Life through me satisfies the Heavenly Father.

Again, I was never asked to be or produce love. We were created to receive it and allow it to pour forth out of us.

*...**present your bodies a living and holy sacrifice**, acceptable to God, which is your spiritual service of worship.*
Romans 12:1 NASB

If I desire more love and devotion for the Father, I have one course of action—ASK. To increase my love and devotion, I just receive more of His Life and Love, since I do have the power of choice. I can choose to ask for more love.

This takes the pressure off my expectations of self. Desire is my divine invitation to Christ's own Life and Love. If I try to produce it myself, all I will be is frustrated. I was never intended to produce love or life, only to present my body for *His*.

So, I accept this divine invitation to receive more of the Life and Love of Christ to pour out on the Father. My despair and desperation to love God more is Jesus' own desire in me. Let it reign, Father, to satisfy Yourself in me!

I made Your name known to them and will make it known, so the love You have loved Me with may be in them and I may be in them.
John 17:26 HCSB

As the Father has loved Me, so have I loved you. Abide in My love. If you keep My commandments, you will abide in My love, just as I have kept My Father's commandments and abide in His love.
John 15:9-10 ESV

Is It Jesus or Not?

When you love the Lord, you will listen for His voice and search out His countenance. We are called to be identifiers, to spiritually discern people and situations. But we are not called to test whether something is good or bad. We are to look for Jesus.

I do not get to decide what is good or evil; this knowledge is way above my paygrade. It is not my job either. The temptation to play God infuses that kind of judging. To live deciding by human reasonings and opinions is to live searching for answers from the Tree of Knowledge. This has always been a big no-no for man. I am to eat from the Tree of Life, which is Christ, the solid root and heavenly stock. This keeps my focus and gaze on Him and not the world.

Lord, my heart is not proud; my eyes are not haughty. I do not get involved with things too great or too difficult for me.

Instead, I have calmed and quieted myself like a little weaned child with its mother; I am like a little child.

Israel, put your hope in the Lord, both now and forever.
Psalm 131 HCSB

Jesus is the deciding variable of ALL of life, not my logic. I am to live as a witness of whether things are Christ, my Beloved, or not. The only thing motivating this is the pursuit of Love. "Do I hear my Beloved, the one that I love?"

Here is what we are *not* to do: try to determine whether situations, people, and circumstances are good or bad. "Is this Christ or not?"—that's the *only* question. "Do I hear the voice of my Shepherd or the voice of another?"

Knowing the answer to this question comes from relationship. If I have no relationship with Jesus Christ, I will have no spiritual discernment. I become acquainted with His Voice, His smell, His heartbeat as I remain dependent on Him. It is through time spent with Jesus that I come to know Him and fall in love. I spend time with Jesus as my Shepherd.

Spiritual discernment has nothing to do with intellect. It is not about head knowledge; it is about Source. And it's about power. If I assume the power to define my world, I will dwell in the mind, not the Spirit.

My spirit listens for Christ's leading. I am to live in the simple wonder of a child, not as a judge. This is freedom and liberty, not ignorance and limitation. The Lord does not burden me with the task of figuring out whether something is good or bad; He frees me to enter into relationship with Him and **to know HIM**. It is our union that makes me aware of the world around me, *not my logic.*

If you know the purpose of all of life, you understand how wondrous this is. Your life is designed to increase your knowledge of Christ; it is not happenstance. It is about relationship and union with Jesus, not circumstance and situations. If you leave that goal and purpose, you leave Christ.

If I occupy myself with the Tree of Good and Evil, then I am in a dialog with the devil. And the only reason I would do this is for *power*. In the Garden it was a struggle for power, and that remains true today. We want the power of knowledge to decide good and bad so we do not have to listen to our Father God.

Here is the truth: the only real power in this life is the power of relationship with Jesus Christ. All other power is illegitimate.

You hem me in, behind and before, and lay Your hand upon me. Such knowledge is too wonderful for me; it is high; I cannot attain it.
Psalm 139:5-6 ESV

God Sees ME!

A big part of relationship is seeing the other person and being seen by them in return. My great Aunt Maizie did that for me. I had the privilege of attending her 100th birthday party some years ago, and though it was quite far away, the Lord asked me to go, so off we went. I drove there so I would have more time with God. His revealed purpose for my trip was to simply say thank you to this beloved great aunt for *seeing me*. It is one thing to spend time with someone, but it is quite another to see them. *Being seen is huge.* To see ***the*** person and not just *a* person is an enormous gift to that individual.

All of us can be with people yet not actually see them. Perhaps we only see what God allows us to see. And when I was a small child, He let Aunt Maizie see *me*. She and I did not spend a lot of time with one another, because she lived quite a distance away. But through the years, we spoke over the phone, and what Maizie said on those calls told me that *she saw me*.

At this party I met many distant relatives I never even knew existed. Typical niceties were exchanged, but essentially, I was thrown into a pool of strangers who happened to be related to me. One of them, a second cousin I think, was a delight. She saw the quandary I was in, and attempted to make this awkward scenario more comfortable. Remember, I was only there to deliver a message to Maizie. But this cousin directed me to a message which validated the whole trip. I was shocked how it played out.

Knowing nothing of my relationship with Maizie or what God had asked me to do, she recommended that I check out some podcasts by a pastor she likes, a man named Erwin McManus. And the random message I chose to listen to was all about "being seen."

> "People are searching for God; they want to see God. But what they need more than anything is to realize that **God** sees them. And the church, when we come together, is the way that God allows Himself to be seen by a world that is looking for Him. We make the Invisible, visible. But more than making it possible for people to see Jesus through us, it is even more important that they are seen by us. That they realize that Jesus sees them because we see them."

"You are the God who sees me!"

She also said, "In this place, have I actually seen the One who sees me?" So that well was named Beer-lahai-roi (which means "well of the Living One who sees me")...
Genesis 16:13b-14a

"You are El Roi—the God who sees me."

By seeing me, Maizie ministered God's value of me, to me. God gave her eyes to see me, and that somehow communicated to me that *God saw me*. I was not aware of it at the time; it was like opening a belated birthday present when He showed me.

The smallest drop of Christ's Life is enough to send ripples across the whole landscape of a life. And where those waves go is beyond our purview.

When I finally spoke with Maizie at her party, she was unaware of her impact on my life. And I think it is exactly how it is supposed to be. Jesus was at the center and His heart was transferred both in the sending and receiving.

Cast your bread upon the waters, for you will find it after many days.
Ecclesiastes 11:1 ESV

The Life of Christ in us is like casting our bread upon the waters. We freely give Him away and then the Gift is gone. Jesus fosters *for Himself* the impact of His Life. Often, it is quite apart from me. Now that I am on this side of my life, I see that others, just like Maizie, *saw me*. And I believe that God sees others through *me*.

I am keenly aware of others, possibly to a fault, because God designed me *to see*. By nature, I am very aware, but my natural proclivity does not bring Life. It is only when Jesus sees through me that it becomes Life.

Before I was saved, my motivation to see was self-saving. I *saw* in order to keep myself safe. It did not work well, but that did not deter me. God gifted me with keen awareness, and I used it for self. But once Jesus had my life, He took control of my seeing.

One of the ways the Lord trained me to see as He sees was through being a shepherd. To shepherd sheep and goats requires great awareness.

Now, I was a city boy and didn't know the first thing about them. What I quickly learned was that you have to see them as if you are seeing yourself. You are the sole support for these animals. They cannot care for themselves, even in the smallest ways. So, I became their awareness of self. I saw their health, afflictions, maladies, and I was their care.

Can you imagine one of the lambs standing up and saying, "I am feeling a little wormy today. Do you mind giving me a little of that herbal formula over there?" Nope, that was mine to see and diagnose. I knew when they were wormy and what to do to rectify it.

I cannot keep myself any more than those sheep could. Just because I can shove food in my face does not mean I can properly care for myself. And I cannot see another if my eyes are firmly affixed on myself.

God trained my eyes to follow His view. And in this way, He trained me to be a shepherd-pastor, too. I cannot see anything God does not show me, but when He is looking through me, I see with such clarity. Before I was saved I saw out of fear, but now that I am His, I see out of His fullness.

So what is the moral of this story? God used Maizie to communicate His message, and the reason she was unaware of her impact is because she was a vessel, not the Source. For me, every interaction with Maizie was an interaction with God. And this is the truth of Christ *in* me, *as* me. Because He is the Source of Life, we often are unaware of who *He* is impacting and how. This is the glory of the exchanged life.

> *God saved you by His grace when you believed. And you can't take credit for this; it is a gift from God. Salvation is not a reward for the good things we have done, so none of us can boast about it. For we are God's masterpiece. He has created us anew in Christ Jesus, so we can do the good things He planned for us long ago.*
> Ephesians 2:8-10 NLT

For the most part, I am completely unaware of Christ's impact through me. This keeps my eyes focused on Him and He gets the total glory for anything He does. This is wonderful for many reasons. One, if I am trying to impact someone, I am less likely to bring Christ purely. If I am focused on them, it is a huge temptation to want to solve or satisfy them. This is just our nature. If we see a need, we often have the desire to fix it. If someone needs a hand, I reach out with mine. But if it is Christ doing things through me, then I am not the one trying to fix, tell, teach, or support… He is the Source.

Another good reason to be grateful that I am unaware of Christ's impact? *No big head*. Even the best of us can be tempted to inflate when ***we*** bring a solution. And there is no need to proclaim it aloud, my inward man can boast all by himself *to himself*. "Look at what I have done!" This statement is usually followed by a raucous crash. What I build inevitably collapses, because flesh is flawed and failing. This is the opposite of what Christ's Life erects, because He is eternal and Life-giving.

I am flabbergasted at how God blows in and out like the wind. "*The wind blows wherever it pleases. You hear its sound, but you cannot tell where it comes from or where it is going. So it is with everyone born of the Spirit*" (John 3:8). Not only is He the wind toward me but also *through* me. Christ interacts with us through many vessels, and engages others through us. He is able to bring His message through whatever or whomever He wishes. We do not know where the Wind is coming from or where He is going.

Jesus bears witness to His own Life and we are His chosen vessels to carry this Life. Through us and towards us He speaks words, gives a hand, or like my great Aunt Maizie, casts a gaze. He is the singular Source of all Life.

Remember, dear brothers and sisters, that few of you were wise in the world's eyes or powerful or wealthy when God called you. Instead, God chose things the world considers foolish in order to shame those who think they are wise. And He chose things that are powerless to shame those who are powerful. God chose things despised by the world, things counted as nothing at all, and used them to bring to nothing what the world considers important. As a result, no one can ever boast in the presence of God.

1 Corinthians 1:26-29 NLT

Having A True Relationship with God

Do you ever find yourself following a formula in pursuit of relationship with God? I think that's very common. We get an idea in our heads what relationship should look like rather than seeking God about it. Perhaps you believe He is only found in scripture reading and study. Or possibly only in quiet moments alone, or while singing in worship. Maybe He is waiting for you in intercessory prayer times or a carefully crafted combination of each of these. These are all wonderful ways to spend time with God. But if the method is made source, then it becomes a spiritual treadmill in lieu of a real relationship with God.

I asked the Lord, "What are You looking for in relationship with me? What is it, God, that *You* desire?"

I am not going to share His full answer to me, because my answer would be different than yours. My answer is mine and mine alone. That is what relationship is: completely individual interaction with another. Which one of us would want a textbook formula in our most personal relationships? Methods are cold and calculated, void of heart. We all want relationships that are natural, free flowing, and *personal.*

I will share one thing that God said in response to my question. One of the major areas where God waits for us is in the working of the cross into our daily lives. He showed me that our relationship is forged in the crushing of my will on my daily cross and the subsequent experience of His Resurrection Life.

Ultimately, relationship with God is simply taking His hand and walking with Him through every moment—painful, exhilarating, angry, loving, sad, joyful, etc. Every moment is to be spent with Him.

Christ went to His cross alone so He could stand with me in mine.

Can All Our Relationships Be IN Christ?

If I had received in my 20s the revelation in this chapter, it would have alleviated a number of painful issues in my life. Now that I am over 50, I would say it is about time to get it. And I am trusting that God's timing has been absolutely perfect in this. May I finally, *truly* get it, and may it help those who read this: For the Christian, there are no true, intimate relationships apart from being ***in Christ***.

Our intimate relationships are *intended* to be Church. This does not mean that we will be sequestered in silence and solitude most of the time, or that we only interact with *the church*. But as Christians, we have *no* true relationships outside of Christ. We will always have acquaintances, associates, and store clerk interactions. We live in this world and interact with people daily, but these are not intimate relationships. I'm referring to deep, intimate, spirit-to-spirit relationship—not common, everyday interactions.

But he replied to the man who told him, "Who is my mother, and who are my brothers?" And stretching out his hand toward his disciples, he said, "Here are my mother and my brothers! For whoever does the will of my Father in heaven is my brother and sister and mother."
Matthew 12:48-50 ESV

I know to some this sounds anti-social, but it is in fact *more* relational not *less*. Martha Kilpatrick once said that she wanted to experience church in her relationships with each of her children. Her choice for their relationship was to be *in* Christ rather than *in* family. This takes it higher than just a mother/child relationship, straight into Body Life.

Martha also spoke of when the Lord confronted her about her relationship with her husband. Jesus said, "You're not his wife; I am his wife *through you*." This is absolutely amazing. This takes "Christ in you" to the heights.

Remember my mantra? "Christ's life as my life is **His** life *in* my life, and that's not my life as His life, it's Him." I have seen that worked out practically in many lives, and I see the wisdom and glory of this.

When all of our relationships are *in* Christ, then all of our knowing is *of* Christ.

Only then do we experience Jesus in every facet of our lives. It becomes an Apostle Paul experience – "that I may know Him." Can you imagine if all of your deepest relationships were about experiencing Christ and His Life?

This does not mean that you remain aloof or remote where people are concerned. You may find that it is quite the opposite when walked out in life.

> *And this, so that I may know Him [**experientially, becoming more thoroughly acquainted with Him, understanding the remarkable wonders of His Person more completely**] and [in that same way experience] the power of His resurrection [which overflows and is **active** in believers], and [that I may share] the fellowship of His sufferings, by being continually conformed [inwardly into His likeness even] to His death [dying as He did].*
> Philippians 3:10 AMP (emphasis mine)

Currently my most intimate and closest relationships are *in* Christ. It is church! I am talking about His transcendent church, which is relationship *in* Christ's own Body. This is a union that is more about relationship with Him than just relating to others. Yet all the while, relating to others is often closer and more intimate than if it were not *in* Christ.

Here is a funny visual about being *in* Christ. My kidney, my liver and my stomach are pretty close. They work in conjunction with each other *in* me. Functionally they are pretty close, but their focus is ultimately me.

This reality has been proven to me over and over again. There is a unity that is experienced in relationships, *in* Christ, that is incredibly deeper than mere human connections. True ***Body life*** is the knowing of Christ as He wishes to reveal Himself in the members of His Body. The result is a bond so beyond commonality and familiarity. It is knowledge of and union with Him and the members of His very own Body. Jesus makes Himself known as He expresses Himself through us. Now that is relationship!

"I renounced, for the love of Him, everything that was not He; and I began to live as if there was none but He and I in the world."[3]
Brother Lawrence 1611-1691

Life is about God first, foremost, and throughout the length of our days. God is at the center of every aspect of our lives, and God is our only source for life. Everything that happens in this life is about God. Every interaction we have is about God. It is about how **He sees** our circumstance and what **He does** within our lives. God is the Source and Focus of every step, every moment, and every interaction.

Early in my Christian life, God spoke this to me:

> "I AM the seamless thread of your entire life. People will come and people will go, but I AM the One constant that includes them all. I AM your beginning

3 The Practice of the Presence of God, Brother Lawrence, Paraclete Press, Copyright 2010.

> and I AM your end. At the finish, all there will be is ME. This life is about Me!"

When I heard this, I was both excited and daunted. Though I loved the fact that God was that involved and engaged with me, it seemed so extreme and unstable. I know that God being THE constant of life is as stable as you get, but to hear that no one else would be there as a constant was disconcerting. Who doesn't want someone in their life to be faithful, constant, and present? But what God was saying to me is that no other person would be my stability; there would be none but God and Him alone.

Am I an isolated case of God's choosing? No, this is the reality for all His children. God is *the* center, and all our dealings are with Him, even if they are directed towards another. **God is *my* great I AM and *all* of my life is about Him.**

After reading Nehemiah one day, I realized that he lived in this reality. Look at his interaction with Artaxerxes. Nehemiah's speaking to the king was unto God, and his interaction with the king was seen as a prayer to God. "With a prayer to the God of heaven, he replied" (to the king). It was a prayer to God because there was none but God in Nehemiah's life. People came and people went, but Nehemiah lived with God. He was aware of God first and foremost. Imagine that line being so clear in your life that even words spoken to your authority would be perceived as to God!

Now, I struggle with making relationships about others or myself all the time. But I have assurance that God is faithful and patient. He will get me where I need to be. God is able to batter my heart unto Himself.

Batter my heart, three-person'd God
By John Donne

Batter my heart, three-person'd God, for you
As yet but knock, breathe, shine, and seek to mend;
That I may rise and stand, o'erthrow me, and bend
Your force to break, blow, burn, and make me new.
I, like an usurp'd town to another due,
Labor to admit you, but oh, to no end;
Reason, your viceroy in me, me should defend,
But is captiv'd, and proves weak or untrue.
Yet dearly I love you, and would be lov'd fain,
But am betroth'd unto your enemy;
Divorce me, untie or break that knot again,
Take me to you, imprison me, for I,
Except you enthrall me, never shall be free,
Nor ever chaste, except you ravish me.

Why Can't We Be Friends?

If you establish a relationship outside of the life of Christ, you are establishing a soulish, fleshly and ultimately Kingdom-distracting union. Does this seem harsh, over the top, or extreme? Ask yourself. Has any relationship that you have made in the flesh ever directly benefited your spiritual life? Has it ever produced the life of the Kingdom? I would have to say no. Yes, God is a miracle worker and can bring forth the purposes of heaven even through my blunders. But that is His grace and graciousness *to me*. Relationships established in the flesh have caused me needless pain and suffering. Suffering I might have avoided if I had stayed *in Christ*.

"Why can't I make relationships when and with whom I want?" Well, we have the right to do so thanks to free will, but just because we *can*, does not mean we *should*. When we were crucified with Christ, our lives ceased to be our own. Christ's Life is my life. My life ended and He now lives His Life through me. Now my life is found in Him, hidden in the heavens. I am to have no further self-interests *because I am no more.*

If I establish a relationship motivated by what I want, then it is selfish and of the flesh. And if it is flesh, then it is sin. "Oh John, you've just gone too far there!" But Jesus Himself said that if you are not for Him, you're against Him. If you're not gathering, you are scattering (Matthew 12:30). Basically, if you are not building the Kingdom, you are tearing it down. And the practicality of this scripture is frightening. It is not just theoretical; it is lived out in every aspect of our lives.

Is this an easy word? Do I like this truth? No, but God has pricked my heart that He alone defines my interactions. My motivation and desire to gain something for self does not obscure the reality in which I speak. My life is Christ's Life now; it is not my life anymore.

Good! Because there is something higher than relationships that serve me. I can experience Jesus within me. I can know Him through my relationships.

This does not mean I will only ever have relationships with believers. No, God leads us to have relationships with unbelievers for various reasons. The point is that these relationships will be *for Jesus,* not self. They will be about His relating rather than my self-serving extractions of need. Have you ever heard someone say of their soul mate, "They complete me!"? This essentially says, "Thank God, I finally found a source for what I was missing and wanted."

Years ago, Martha talked about Isaiah 48:12 – I am He, I am the First, I am also the Last. The Hebrew translation is *Ani-hi* and *harishon af ani haaharon*, which means, "An 'I-He' [a union between me and Him] is the first, and an 'I' [which is only I] is the last." This can be a little confusing, but also absolutely amazing. First I come into union with Christ, and then He becomes all there is.

St. Gertrude prayed: "I am You. You are I. I am not You, You are not I. I and You, we are a new being: an I-You."[4]

I am a New Creation: Jesus-in-me!

Dragging my Frankenstein-monster-self out of the grave only produces death and destruction. My self-life exhumed seeks to destroy that which is glorious—the Life of Christ now indwelling my body. The repercussions of seeking relationships for self are just not worth it. Experiencing Christ's relationships through my body is so fulfilling. It's amazing to know more of Him.

Living for the Audience of ONE

I was present when a dear friend of mine, Yvonne Peters, delivered a message called the *Audience of One*. At the time, it skewered me because someone had put into words, with a visual picture, a message I had been resisting most of my life.

Yvonne is a professional dancer and choreographer. For years she directed the pageantry and worship at the Feast of the Tabernacles in Jerusalem, Israel. I have to say, I have never seen her dance when I have not been drawn into that worship myself. She expresses the heart of deep worship with the movements of her body. And it is beautiful to see.

Yvonne related a dream she had. She was in an empty theater where she was practicing a dance before going into a worship event. After some time, she noticed a man towards the back of the theater sitting all alone. She entreated him to come to an adjacent area where there were tons of worshippers worshipping. At this point, the man revealed Himself as the Lord. He asked her one of those simply piercing questions which the Lord loves to pose:

"Would you be willing to dance just for Me?"

I have had many similar questions from the Lord. I know that they are not uncommon to His children. But His recurring question of me is, "Will you live for My pleasure alone? Will you do it just for Me?" I am aware of some of the blessings in this calling. I can also see the benefit of accepting this call to solitude, but it is not without sacrifice.

As a child, I reluctantly lived a solitary life. I was an only child and a bit awkward. I had few friends and found myself alone more often than not.

After I became a Christian in my early 20s, the Lord asked me if I would remain single for Him. Though my preference was always to have a wife and children, I did say yes. It was a huge death. I will more extensively go into this in the next section, but for now, Yvonne's dream deeply impacted me because my life was set for an audience of One.

God laid a foundation of circumstances to bridle me into a calling: "Will you do it for Me alone?" In living this out, I have felt the ache of loneliness and the pain of neglect. But the pain lessened the more I believed in Jesus Christ—His choosing of me, His pleasure in me, and His presence round about me.

Though I have at times resisted my solitary life, that resistance only made me susceptible to attack. Yet each blow has been the Lord helping me to fulfill my call. His whispering voice continually stirs my pot: "Would you do it just for Me even if you see no other fruit?"

I made the ultimate choice of YES long ago, but sometimes I am asked to reaffirm my commitment. Each of us in varying degrees knows this call. The Lord is a jealous God and He asks each of us, "Will you do it for Me alone?" While everything in the world calls us to socialize with and perform for the masses, God remains in the back of the theater as our true audience of One.

I am my Beloved's, and His desire is for me.
Songs 7:10 ESV

Where was God in My Story of The Great Exchange?

The more I abide in Christ, the more I can live beyond the way I think my life should be to find joy in what already is.

Unknown

Thus far, I have painted a picture of the struggle to live the exchanged Life. I have illustrated the difference between the old nature and the new man, and have shown what it looks like to enter the Sabbath Rest. I have revealed the reward of saying YES to God and the power of every choice we make. And while I have given examples along the way, I now want to share with you a deeper testimony of how Christ made my own life about His Life.

This is one of the greatest gifts I can entrust to you. I lay bare my own personal Great Exchange in the hope that it will encourage your own. The true power we carry as born-again believers is in the impartation of Christ's Life by the revealing of that very Life in us. I pray you are blessed by my testimony!

The Tangible Touch of God

Throughout most of my life, I tried to extract love from God, to get Him to express His love for me in a way that I could *feel*. Especially in moments of depression, stress, or fear, I wanted Him to display His love to me. I looked for a *tangible touch*—a confirmation of His love. I have wondered if this is a rare thought among Christians, or if I am simply just one of many. I do not know, it seems somehow to be like sacrilege to mention it. As if it were a betrayal to the One who proves His love over and over again, with the ultimate Gifts of His Son's Life and His indwelling Spirit. But at the end of the day, I wanted God to touch me.

I sought the Lord, crying out for much of my life, "Where are You?" I ran about to many charismatic Christian conferences and meetings looking for His touch. I was hungering for something that I could *experience*. In these meetings, the Spirit would apparently touch many around me and leave me untouched. I once had a friend joke with me that I was an "oak of righteousness," meaning I stood like a tree when the Wind came rather than falling under His presence. But though I smiled, this was never funny to me. I left these meetings often in tears, feeling disappointed and rejected. "What is wrong with me, God? Why don't you touch *me*?"

Is this you? Have you experienced this, too? Well, I want to share what I have learned. I want to tell some of my story, and open up some of the *whys* which He has revealed to me. My prayer is that we will all see more of God by the end.

Where Are You, God?

If life was a corridor and I were to look back down my hall, one of my through-lines would be the question, **"Where are You, God?"** Even as a very young child, I looked for God. I had an innate pursuit of Him. I wanted to touch Him and to be touched by Him. I do not say this with any sense of pride, as if I was some sort of prodigy, because I now realize it had little to do with me. (And really, everywhere I could possibly do it wrong, I did.) My hunger for God was simply His own grace and calling of me. I would find out, as time passed, just what the purpose of this hunger was.

I Love My Life

When I was just under four years old, I had an encounter with God that has marked my whole life. There was a church bus that pulled up directly in front of our house every Sunday morning. I do not know how I did this, but one day I hopped up on it with the rest of the kids without my mother's knowledge.

I have no memory of the trip to the church or how I got into my seat in the sanctuary, but I do remember listening intently to the pastor. During his sermon, I learned two things. First, that we all were going to die—*life would end*. And second, that if you loved your life, you would lose it, and if you hated your life, you would have it eternally. I remember saying to God in response, "**But I love my life!**" The words of this pastor have never left me, though I have resisted them all of my life.

Chasing God's Love

Through age 7, I would write little notes to God, run outside, toss them into the air, and then quickly run back into the house. I was hungry to connect with Him. I was a very tactile child with wide-open senses, and I deeply yearned for a touch. I was not raised in a religious home; I was just looking for God. Well into my late teens, I would go to churches after hours and enter the empty sanctuaries, crying out, "God, where are You?!" I was desperate – life had battered me as it does everyone – and I needed Him to come. I could never figure out why He did not meet my passionate pursuit by satisfying **ME** and my desires. And as I ruminated over that through the years, what was once a child's plea became a louder adult demand. I wanted Him to move, to be real, and to show His love to me!

I actually became bitter with God in my preteen years, a condition I suffered from for quite a while. Because He did not come to me in the way I desired, I translated that as His rejection. Satan's lie that God was withholding from me something I NEEDED attached itself to His apparently deferred answer (Prov. 13:12).

An Ultimatum

Bitterness is rottenness to the bone. In anger, I tried to find an alternative to God's love, but it was not there. Everything that promised satisfaction just left me emptier and emptier. I was set on a path to find Him, and it was Him I had to find.

When I was twenty, I was living in a van, and God came a-knocking. (The details of these events are found on CD #3 of the Love Reigns Shulamite Ministries conference.) God confronted my bitterness with an ultimatum: **"You are either going to live for Me, or I am going to take you out!"** Though this was not my first audible hearing of God, it was His most direct. By this point in my life's journey, I was no longer merely desiring God's touch, I was now LOUDLY demanding it with complete entitlement. I responded to the King of Glory, my Creator, with, "Well, that's not much of a choice." I felt betrayed before His ultimatum, and now I felt put upon. I guess if I was cognizant, I would have said, "Okay, let me get this straight. I've sought You for 20 years and here on this 20th day of March, You come and say, 'My Way or the highway?!'" Though I did not give a resounding YES! to God's warning, the weak but affirmative response I did give caused everything in my life to be different.

Saved Yet Still Searching for God

Over the next year, God slowly extracted me from my quagmire of rebellion. He cleaned up the externals and lit a new fire in my heart that His touch would be realized. During that year, I did actually get saved and start going to a seeker-friendly church. The messages were fresh and alive to me. I was so excited. Finally, I found a place that spoke about a relationship with God. But after a few years, the rotation of entertaining messages started to wear thin, and I began to again say to God, "Where are You?"

I followed one of the pastors when he started a new church that he said would experience an Acts-like Pentecost. But after being there for an additional few years, I finally spoke up and said, "Um, where's the beef? We aren't experiencing Pentecost; this is just the same stuff in a new building." So off I went in search of the tangible touch of God. I now had a new life and heart, but I still did not have the intimacy I was yearning for with the Lord.

No Counterfeit for Me

I was searching for God in the charismatic movement. If there was any kind of "glory" meeting that promised the manifest presence of God, I was there. I was hungry for His touch and willing to travel to find it.

Though the masses were slain in the Spirit at these meetings, I was left standing alone, the so-called "oak of righteousness." This rang the bell of my previous heart-hopes, now deferred again, making me sick (Prov. 13:12).

I had a genuine passion to experience God and I wanted an *actual experience*. I was not prepared to lie about receiving something that I did not; I would not violate my own conscience that way. Though I might have been willing to sell myself for some counterfeit, I was not going to make it up or work myself into it. Funny enough, God was not up for my settling for counterfeit either, so I just stood as people all around me fell out.

I was not doing this for others; I was doing this for **ME**. I was not seeking to save face in front of people. This was my long-time pursuit, one that had arrested me as a young child. So among the Toronto Blessings, Rodney Howard Brown meetings, Brownsville Revivals and the like, I sought God.

Increasing My Spiritual Capacity

Usually I left these meetings in tears, or in anger, because the Spirit did not touch me in the way He seemed to touch others. I said to Him as I left these meetings, "What is it about me that You don't like?" A deep-seated spirit of rejection and fear of abandonment played with my emotions like a cat with a mouse. So I left these meetings with the Accuser, who was accusing God of withholding from me something I NEEDED.

I am not saying God abused me in this; not one day of my life has He abused me. Often I have equated pain with something must be wrong. If I hurt, it must be off. If something is hurting you, fix it, right? No, though God was willing to hurt me, it was for an amazing plan and purpose.

God is so incredibly trustworthy with our hearts. He works things together for us with skill and intricacy. And signs of hunger are not evidence of error. My Creator was working into my heart an increased spiritual capacity to experience Him. He was stretching my ability to experience, and this had to be done through hunger pains and His resistance to my demands. You do not demand to move into a house when only the foundation is set. No, you wait until the Builder builds the dwelling and sets things in order.

...And He answered and said, "It is not good to take the children's bread and throw it to the dogs." But she said, "Yes, Lord; but even the dogs feed on the crumbs which fall from their masters' table." Then Jesus said to her, "O woman, your faith is great; it shall be done for you as you wish." And her daughter was healed at once.
Mathew 15:26-28 NASB

Martha Kilpatrick has taught me that the size of the hunger is the size of the fulfillment. In my "NOW!" generation, delayed gratification is seen as abusive. But God is unmoved. He is working together a purpose and fulfillment that is His to bestow. This Canaanite woman was willing to do something I failed to do: humble her*self* and take the lowest place. I had my demands of God but not the humility to bow. I had always seen Jesus' interaction with this woman as cruel . . . *I wonder why*! Jesus wanted to increase her hunger to fulfill His choice of satisfaction. She was willing to bow. I, on the other hand, had to receive a few more knocks against my pride.

Maybe you can relate to my story? Maybe you have scampered about looking for that legitimate, undeniable touch from your God. Has God withheld from you to increase your spiritual capacity?

Will You Marry Me?

After years of seeking God *on my terms*, I felt like I was being stretched for endurance and capacity. Yet God met my desire with a question: "Will you marry Me?"

A Hard Proposal

I was driving from Atlanta to St. Simons Island to pick up something for Martha, and that trip is grueling. You kind of feel like you are in a film loop. All you see for hours is the same thing—flat, hot, green nothing. On the drive down, the Lord blew my mind. He asked me a question and I heard the words: "Will you remain single for Me?"

These words evoked in me a wave of emotion. First of all, I wanted a wife and children. I had even been picked out of my congregation, unprompted, by a few people who prophesied over me—"Soon you will be getting married!" So my first response to God's proposal was to be crushed.

I wept for hours as I drove through that green wasteland. I had to count the cost of my answer. Marital and familial desires would have to die upon my answer of yes. I would be seen as an oddity among Christendom, which bows at the altar of marriage. People would assume I was not sexually whole. I would have to face life being often solitary, a dread I faced regularly as an only child. The question, "Then who will I grow old with?" shook some deep level of inner security.

Next came the obligations I was under. My parents always wanted grandchildren, for a start, and the list went on and on. All I knew was that my answer was not allowed to be a "Yes" followed by "*Just kidding*." God was asking me to give Him something that would mark me for the rest of my life.

Toward the end of my drive, I finally gave God my answer. "Yes, I will remain single for You." And I have to be honest, there was a motive for self in this. When I realized what I would be giving up for Him, I thought about what I would gain. I figured that if I gave all of this to Him, maybe it was because He had a deeper plan for my life. And just maybe, the plan was that I would be married to *Him*. I thought, "Now I will have the intimacy I have desired with You!" So the tears were turned into joy. Why would God ask me to give Him something and not fill the void with Himself?

I must tell you that I do believe God has done just that and this *is* my reality now, but that too happened *on His terms*.

Beach Blanket Bingo

I am now going to share a part of my testimony that is very private. I only do this because I feel like this story is "His-story." I do not own it; it is God's authoring of His Life in my life.

Upon arriving at St. Simons Island on that fateful trip, I began to plan a date night with God. I figured if He was asking me to be single for Him, then it was His to fill in the gap. So I set up a night that was just for us. I went to a remote beach and sat in plain view of a wonderful lighthouse. My heart was palpitating and I was a bit nervous, like playing beach blanket bingo or something. I had sought God's tangible touch all my life and now I was going to *feel* it.

Let me say here that I had experienced the manifest presence of God before that night. I had audibly heard Him several times, even as an unsaved youth. I had experienced Him with my senses in episodes, like where He confronted me in the van. But I had not had

Him touch me. I am a man with heightened senses—I hear things keenly, I smell things acutely, I taste things intensely. My senses are WIDE awake. In Florida, where I lived as a child, I spent hours in the pool because I loved the way water felt. I have always been this way; it is just how God made me.

I have always wanted to be touched, yet God Himself set things up in my life so that my physical contact with others would be minimal. I did not have brothers to wrestle with, or even many friends with whom to pal around. But just because my reality was set a certain way, it did not lessen any of my desires. I wanted what I was not given. So when God asked me to lay down a further stake of my hopes being satisfied, it was a death. But what came with it was a grand hope of fulfillment in return.

So there I sat, waiting for the Spirit of the Living God. Yet after hours of waiting without so much as a breeze, I finally picked up my stuff and wept my way to the car. I was crushed. He did not come as I had desired. Eyes filled with tears, I sat in the car for quite a while just asking God what it was He wanted from me. Why would He not bow to ME?! Okay, that is not what I *said*, but it certainly was what I was *saying*.

The next day I wondered what that was all about as I made the journey back home. One thing I did know, I was the Lord's. **But was He mine?** I know many people who seek the Lord to be their romance. I think it is naked humanity to desire Him as *our* ultimate fulfillment. But I believe we can take this to the stratosphere of self-worship—where I want God to worship me and bow to me as center. Since the Garden, we have wanted to control Him to do our will, so we will be pleased. He just is not interested in playing in that arena.

Juiced That Sucker Off

As I shared at the *Reign of the Kingdom* Shulamite Ministries conference, I had a dramatic encounter with God while recovering from slicing off the end of my finger. Yeah, I accidentally took off the end of my index finger on my left hand while using a juicer. It was a shocking event that has become *very holy* to me. Why? Because of what God revealed to me through it. As Martha can attest, I walked in a supernatural grace all the way through this situation. I drove myself to the hospital, I went through the two surgeries needed to rebuild my finger, and survived the weeks of pain and recovery with inexplicable joy and peace.

Funny thing about the whole encounter, I did not know all that the Lord had done until I was preparing to share this experience with everyone at the conference. But what happened was astonishing. Christ Himself entered into a place of deep fear in my heart so that He could worship the Father *in that dark space.*

As I had developed bitterness with God during my childhood, mostly for not performing as I would have liked, I also became a deeply fearful person. (I am wondering now how linked fear and bitterness are.) I was afraid of death in everything. My life was marked with fear. Illness and injury particularly terrified me, because they all lead to death, right? Who does not feel that lump in their body and not question if it was cancer?

I did not have God in this place of fear, and I was paralyzed in it. This area was a deep hole of darkness where Satan had the right to torment me. And who would not be terrified by losing a part of their body? But God in His wonderful wisdom knew just how to address this. **Christ entered my dark place of fear and explosively worshiped the Father in it.** This has blown my mind! There was no worship of the Father in this area of my life and this incident with my finger gave Him entrance to fill it with His Light.

In the end, it was not comfort that I needed, it was the Light of His Worship. It completely involved me, but it was not about me. The focus was not my finger, it was worship of the Father. In *my wisdom* I would have directed God to get me out of pain and heal me quickly, but what transpired was the bursting forth of the Son's worship of the Father in my dark place. Humanly this is so counter-intuitive, but it has changed my entire perspective on my passion to be touched by God.

Explosive Worship

> *And we have the prophetic word [made] firmer still. You will do well to pay close attention to it as to a lamp shining in a dismal (squalid and dark) place, until the day breaks through [the gloom] and the Morning Star rises (comes into being) in your hearts.*
> 2 Peter 1:19 AMP

A beloved friend shared 2 Peter 1:19 with me. It is exactly what happened during my finger episode—"Within my dismal and squalid place, Christ, the Morning Star, rose in my heart." The *New Living* translates it this way:

> *Because of that experience, we have even greater confidence in the message proclaimed by the prophets. You must pay close attention to what they wrote, for their words are like a lamp shining in a dark place—until the Day dawns, and Christ the Morning Star shines in your hearts.*

> *Christ rose up in my heart to bring forth worship where* **no** *worship was present. He entered my squalid place of fear and torment with the Light of His own worship for the Father. Imagine, Christ Himself came into my heart to be the worship where I was bound and unable*

to worship. **This worship was not for me nor was it about me, but it completely included me.** *I experienced Christ's own union with and adoration of His Father within my frame.*

I pray that they will all be one, just as You and I are one—as You are in Me, Father, and I am in You. And may they be in Us so that the world will believe You sent Me. I have given them the glory You gave Me, so they may be one as We are one. I am in them and You are in Me. May they experience such perfect unity that the world will know that You sent Me and that You love them as much as You love Me.
John 17:21-23 NLT

I want to bring this point home before I proceed with my story, because this was a pivot in my whole concept of worship and a dynamic turning point in my life. I was not lying in bed with my injured finger, singing songs and hymns. I was not even yielding and surrendering to His Will and perfection in this event. No, I literally was indwelt by the Son of God, who worshiped His Father in me.

After hearing of Christ's worship in my heart, a lovely lady asked, "What did it look like?" Oh, how refreshing that was! It was not sympathy for God taking me on a painful path; instead, it was the child-like wonder of a fascinated heart: "*Tell me!*"

I do not remember how exactly I answered her, but I can say that the worship was explosive. It was loud and big and exuberant. It was far beyond me singing with my eyes closed and hands raised. Christ's worship in me was beyond anything I had even seen or known as worship. It was complete, total, unrelenting focus, with passion and power beyond anything I could muster. The Father and Son were ONE *in me*!

Life Imparted

Another time I recounted these events, my uncle made the statement that all testimony is prophecy. I think he is absolutely correct. I understand it this way. All *real* testimony is of the **Life of Christ** and Life begets Life. So when we testify of the Life of Christ, His Life is imparted. To testify of Christ is literally to prophesy His Life into those who receive.

My earnest prayer is that as I continue to share my story of His Life, the prophetic nature of that Life – the living impartation of Christ – would impact all those reading it.

For the testimony of Jesus is the spirit of prophecy.
Revelation 19:10b NKJV

For the substance (essence) of the truth revealed by Jesus is the spirit of all prophecy [the vital breath, the inspiration of all inspired preaching and interpretation of the divine will and purpose, including both mine and yours].
Revelations 19:10b AMP

Entering a New Reality

After my finger episode, my eyes were opened to a different reality. I saw all my seeking for a tangible touch from God being trumped by my experiencing Christ **as worship**. I am *not* saying that praise and worship is not valid—it is beautiful and brings us, His body, together to focus our gaze on our God with adoration of Him. But I *am* saying that my perspective on worship changed.

I had struggled with praise for years. I felt most was canned, formulaic, and man-centered. It just felt off key. What was called worship in Christendom left me empty most of the time. But plain and simple, maybe my motivation for worship was to offer *baksheesh* to God, so that He would be pleased with me and come and touch me. He was not interested in my bribe, however. He would not be manipulated by my attempts to sweet-talk Him. No, in my life He made sure it was going to be His way alone.

I do worship traditionally, using music to praise God. But it is His movement and anointing that I seek. My consistent question is, "Where are *You* resting?" I have listened to a single song over and over for days if the Spirit of the Living God rested on it. I would rather sit in silence than to attempt to force something. And my experience of Christ during my injury upped the ante in how I seek Him.

I am not saying I still do not seek to experience God's touch, because that would be a lie. I absolutely want Him to express His love to me in a tangible way. It is just that my understanding of what that might look like has been broadened. Where before I tried to extract love from God – especially in moments of depression, stress, or fear. After the juicing episode that changed.

Loving God

I had the thought then, "Wow, why don't I seek to focus my attention on *loving God* rather than a self-centered seeking to **BE** loved by Him?" I know this is not novel but it was foreign to my way of thinking. I think somewhere in my thoughts I figured, "He is God. He has everything and knows everything – I am the needy one here!" *But that is not the whole picture.*

First, I have something He is unable to receive anywhere else in all of creation—my love. I am the only one who can give it. It is my gift and it is solely mine to bestow. He cannot acquire it anywhere else. So if I withhold it from Him, He will never receive it.

Second, and more importantly, *satisfaction in love is to give not receive.* I know this stomps on many wounds – including my own – but it is just true. It is the very nature of love. One (and I do mean ONE) of the reasons divorce runs rampant is because we have tons of broken people all looking to **BE** loved. Love is not for the purpose of acquisition – love yearns to give. There is no growth in simply receiving love. Character and dignity comes from loving, not in being loved.

Though being loved can heal us, it is when love pours out of us that we see real growth and maturing. I always assumed that the scripture, "*It is more blessed to give than receive,*" (Acts 20:35) concerned only physical gifts. What I have discovered is the best gift to give is love!

> *"You shall love the Lord your God with all your heart and with all your soul and with all your strength and with all your mind, and your neighbor as yourself."*
> Luke 10:27 ESV

Two Stories of Love

I want to share two stories of God's expressed love in my life that greatly impacted me. I pray they do the same for you.

Playing Catch with Dad

I was a children's pastor for years. And as the children grew up and left the children's church, I stayed with them and became a youth pastor of sorts. It was a natural progression and dear to my heart. Children's ministry is like giving water to little sponges, but ministry to a teen is so much different. Wounds and the world take a toll on us by the time we become teenagers. I noticed the door of entrance did not open as quickly or widely, if it opened at all.

A young man in his late teens came to our church around this time, and God gave me love for him. To protect his privacy, let's call him Tim. I was wide open to Tim and a relationship immediately sparked. Because of his living circumstances, I knew the time we would have together would be brief, so I availed myself to him as much as possible.

One day Tim asked if I wanted to go out to the park to play catch. I really did not want to, but for his sake, I said okay.

To give you a little background, I was never into sports. As a child, my self-esteem was too damaged to open myself up to the possibility of further ridicule, and I did not go beyond Gray-Y (YMCA youth sports) and Little League. "Hey batter, batter!" felt too much like mockery with the wounds I already had, so my sports career was short.

Tim and I went out to an open field and started tossing the ball. We just talked while the ball lobbed back and forth between us. I wore sunglasses, since I was facing the sun, and I was glad for this because something remarkable happened to me. God flooded in on me and I just started to cry. I never let this young man know I was crying, but the tears poured out of my eyes. I could have sobbed at the power of God's presence, but I allowed the tears to be the only evidence.

Internally I asked God, "What are You doing?" His response was, "Playing catch with you." This was more than I could take. Tim, who I thought I was ministering to, was a pure vessel of God's love for *me*. I do not know if he even had a clue of what was going on. Though we only met a time or two after, God used this afternoon with Tim to heal something deep in my heart.

I did not really have the "playing catch" moments with my dad. It may have been because I was unwilling to be vulnerable to possible scorn. Not that my dad would have done that, but I was just a raw nerve back then. To be really good at something, you have to be willing to fail, and I felt like such a failure already that I simply could not take it in another arena.

So that sunny afternoon I played catch with Dad (the living God), present in a young man who may or may not have had any idea. We stayed out there until dark, and for me it was time with my Father. God desired to play catch with me, something I would not have asked for nor even wanted—but oh, how I loved it.

Building with Jesus the Carpenter

My second story is about Jesus the Carpenter coming to build a barn with me. I had recently moved up to the North Georgia mountains and really felt like God was calling me to get goats. At the time, I had nowhere to pen them up, so I had to build a barn. As I was researching things, I met a guy named Chandler and we became friends. His mother had a small working farm, and to a lesser degree, I was trying to build the same on my property. I went over to check out their set-up and loved what they had done. So I designed a barn that would house both my chickens and goats. It was fully functional, with a milking station, roost and laying box area, vet workshop, feed and hay storage section, and tool shed. It was awesome! I still kind of marvel at it—and here is why.

Chandler came to me one day and said, “I would like to help you build this barn.” I asked him how much he would charge me, and he replied, “No, no, I just want to help you!” This floored me. I thought, “You do?”

We proceeded to lay out the foundation and get the lumber, using Chandler’s tools, truck, and tractor. It was long hours of building a barn from the ground up. I was in awe of this whole thing, because I knew something was happening beyond just building a barn. It was not until one day when I looked up at Chandler fastening down tin on the roof that I saw clearly. It was not Chandler at all—it was Jesus.

Jesus had worked with me day after day as the Carpenter. I do not even know if Chandler was saved, but there he was with Christ’s message – “I want to build this barn with you.” The whole time we had been working, I had a kind of cloud around me. I realized in that moment that it was Christ’s presence.

Never did I have anyone jump in and work with me like that. Though my father was a homebuilder, I did not have any training with hammer and nail. I was maintaining the best I could, and new horizons were daunting. But here was Christ, the Carpenter, taking on the task shoulder to shoulder with me, working with me. Jesus

Himself wanted to do this with me, and He would use whomever He chose to make it happen.

Christ Is In All Things

What relevance do these two stories have to anyone but me? I think they are real life examples of "not I but Christ." I always thought "not I but Christ" was a work of my surrendering and getting out of the way. I believed somehow that it was the effort to choose. I want to tell you, I believe differently now.

I have been crucified with Christ; it is no longer I who live, but Christ lives in me; and the life which I now live in the flesh I live by faith in the Son of God, who loved me and gave Himself for me.
Galatians 2:20 NKJV

It was not Chandler, but Christ who built the barn with me. It was not Tim playing catch with me, but Christ. When we are *in* Christ, Christ becomes ***all things***, not only in us, but also *for* us. Neither of these men was particularly godly, but because I was God's, so were they. I have viewed this scripture very narrowly in the past, but when I asked God to open it up to me, He brought both stories to mind.

These two stories express how Jesus is able to manifest Himself to His own, even through the unwitting. Yes, since my life is hidden in Him and now I am seated with Him in the heavenlies, I experience all things ***in*** Him. "Not I but Christ" runs the gamut of my life. I bless Him that He is unhindered by anything because He is in **ALL THINGS!**

For everything was created by Him, in heaven and on earth, the visible and the invisible, whether thrones or dominions or rulers or authorities—all things have been created through Him and for Him. He is before all things, and by Him all things hold together.
Colossians 1:16-17 HCSB

No Greater Gift

At this point you might say this whole thing is a story of the exchanged Life. And you would be completely correct. I see that my entire life has been for the purpose of knowing Christ. Everything that happened was all about Jesus manifesting His Life and Will in my life. From the beginning until now, my life is about His Life. The process has either been about getting me out of the way or directly expressing His Life through me. And this, dear reader, is the Lord's intent for you as well. Once you have your purpose defined and refined in your heart and mind, the difficult or tedious circumstances pale in importance.

Here is the crazy part of all this. In writing an autobiographical cross section of my life, I am not only falling deeper in love with Jesus but also with myself. I know this sounds strange, but through all of this I am getting a bird's eye view of me as well as Him.

In the middle of our circumstances we can get bogged down in the minutiae. The pain that emanates from our difficulties can be absorbing and overwhelming. In the moment, we can be blinded to all other realities. But when we step back and look at the whole, life can be wondrous and even magical. Apparently the old cliché "hindsight is 20/20" is actually true. And with this 20/20 vision, I see more of the love than the pain. I see myself as fearfully and wonderfully made, and made so by an awe-inspiring and wondrous God.

Imagine the life of a nail. It lives crammed in a box with hundreds of other nails. Then that nail is yanked from that box to be creamed on the head by a huge hammer. It is wedged deep inside a plank of wood where only the tip of its hammered head sees the light of day. Now imagine that after some time passes, this nail is told that it is part of a magnificent mansion. The nail discovers that it isn't a solo entity but part of an amazing whole. This is how it has been for me. This reflective exercise has caused me to love God, as well as myself, that much more.

You have just finished reading a simple cross section of my testimony, not an exhaustive presentation of my life. I did this in order to present a concise view of the essence of my life. Sure, I could have given more detail. I could've described my years as a shepherd, my life at Shulamite Ministries, or gone into greater detail on any of the many aspects of my daily walk with Christ. The events I have shared with you were chosen because each exemplified to me what it is to live an exchange of lives.

His Life as our life is how we experience Heaven on earth. It is not without trials and testing, but it is a knowing of Christ that eclipses any other ministry. To have Jesus live His Life through you is to experience the greatest intimacy humanly possible.

It is my earnest prayer that you do not leave this section thinking only of my experience. I hope you are led to deeper thoughts about your own. Though I gave examples of my life, this exchange of lives is not about just me. It is about Christ's intent and desire for each of us. I believe you have read this because you, too, are not only *designed* to experience Christ's Life as your life but *destined* for this as well.

How The Great Exchange Brings Us into Deep Intimacy

We have no power from God unless we live in the persuasion that we have none of our own.

John Owen
(British church leader, theologian and academic administrator, 1616-1683)

My Life Found in the Life of the Son

"Christ in me" is a huge paradox. Jesus did not unplug me when He came to be me. I am not somehow expunged and it is just Jesus wearing my face. His Life in me is the mystery of the Gospel and my hope of glory, but it does not override another amazing gift of the Father: free will. Free will is choice and God secured this right for me. Why? Because while a slave (which I once was) is conscripted, a son (which I now am) is made willing.

Even with Christ's Life as my life, I still have free will. I have a choice every step of the way—Jesus or me. While my sonship is found in the Life of the Son of God, I, too, am His child and the Spirit in me calls God, "Abba, Father." There is only ONE Son, but God has many children. And when I say yes to the Life of the Son in me, I am in *His* sonship. This only happens when I will be a child, believing the unbelievable and simply receiving the wonder.

...to redeem those under the law, so that we might receive adoption as sons. And because you are sons, ***God has sent the Spirit of His Son into our hearts, crying, "Abba, Father!"*** *So you are no longer a slave but a son, and if a son, then an heir through God.*
Galatians 4:5b-7 HCSB

All those led by God's Spirit are God's sons. For you did not receive a spirit of slavery to fall back into fear, but you received the Spirit of adoption, ***by whom*** *we cry out, "Abba, Father!" The Spirit Himself testifies together with our spirit that we are God's children, and if children, also heirs—heirs of God and coheirs with Christ—seeing that we suffer with Him so that we may also be glorified with Him.*
Romans 8:14-17 HSCB

Though in my neurotic nature I may wish to escape the responsibility, I still have to choose. Christ wants to be me, *with* me. He wants me to choose Him again and again over self. This is relationship; I am NOT eradicated. Jesus wants me to choose to be with Him, and to say yes to Him performing my life. But I always have the free will to do it on my own at any point. This is the choice to live dead or not – a choice we all make daily.

Living dead is not living independently of God; it is living *dependent on Him alone*. To live independently is to live through self-effort or irresponsibility. In irresponsibility, I shrug things off as if it is not my problem. Self-effort involves trying to do everything my way, in my own strength. Either way, I am living independently of Christ, which is death.

In a life dependent on God, you will witness the Life of the Son doing it all. I choose to let Jesus BE my life, and I get to see that wondrous Life up close and personal. What a gift to see Christ live through us! But this only comes as we surrender to the dependence of a child – "not my will but Yours be done."

Sonship!

I wondered how the Spirit functioned in John 17:21. If it is the Godhead, then that is Father, Son *and* Holy Spirit. Well, ask and you shall receive. After sharing my revelation of what church is with Martha, she gave me the answer in the following scripture:

> *For [the Spirit which] you have now received [is] not a spirit of slavery to put you once more in bondage to fear, but you have received the Spirit of adoption [the Spirit producing **sonship**] in [the **bliss** of] which we cry, **Abba (Father)! Father!***
> Romans 8:15 AMP

It is the Spirit who cries, "Abba, Father" *in* us. He is the Spirit of adoption as well as my *cry to be a son*! It is the Spirit who cries out to be a son in me. Martha then told me, "The Father began and created it, the Son finished it, and the Spirit makes it real in and to us." WOW! Not only is this Church, but it is also sonship.

Remember me saying that the worship is not for me nor is it about me, but it completely included me? This is how I am included: I am made a son ***in Christ's*** Sonship. The Spirit of adoption produces His sonship in my frame.

And because you [really] are [His] sons, God has sent the [Holy] Spirit of His Son into our hearts, crying, Abba (Father)! Father!
Galatians 4:6 AMPC

I have gazed at the Father as He is revealed *His story* through me, and in doing so, I have been very surprised by what He's brought forth. Not only is He giving my back story, He's also showing me why my path took the turns it did.

Sonship is a reality that the Father has been birthing in me for years. While I yearned for the Father's touch, He has gone way beyond a mere touch to reveal sonship. What started out as writing down some of my testimony has exploded into the fellowship of the Godhead in my very own body, which is Church. In this is a testimony beyond mere human story. It is a testament of Christ's very Life.

*For in Him the whole fullness of Deity (the Godhead) continues to dwell in bodily form... And you are in Him...[**in Christ you too are filled with the Godhead**—Father, Son and Holy Spirit—and reach full spiritual stature].*
Colossians 2:9-10 AMPC

Attaining to Sonship

One of my favorite messages is on the topic of sonship. It was delivered by Art Katz in June, 2002, at Challis, Idaho, and it was titled *Attaining to Sonship*. This message irrevocably changed my life. I have truly never been the same since that day in June. Amazingly, the reverberation of this word affects my life daily even now. The message was on Sonship, and it *was not* one I merely listened to; its powerful anointing *dynamically* impacted me. Art was an amazing man – a true force of nature. Plain and simple, God used him to impact His world, and I miss him!

We are never going to receive or experience Sonship merely by listening to a teaching on the subject. Sonship comes through *impartation* from the resurrected Life in another. Revelation of the resurrected Life is for understanding, but the reality of it in our lives comes about through an impartation.

The resurrected Life is received and conceived, not perceived.

With rare exceptions, living the resurrected Life of the Son comes through impartation as someone else lives that Life before you. When I heard Art's message, it was a Ground Zero moment in my spiritual life. Everything changed after that. But unseen was the preparation of the Spirit that came first.

I had walked for years with Martha Kilpatrick, who gave daily evidence to the resurrected Life. She was teaching me while being an example of it, and I was receiving it through a living impartation. Martha was living the resurrected Life before me, and I was being changed with each moment of discipleship. God used her to work this message into the soil of my heart, so that when I heard Art speak that day, the reality was ignited in me.

You see, the message itself was not the reality. I know that Art's words that day were not Art but Christ. He was giving witness to the message Christ spoke through him. Art brought forth Sonship reality in delivering a message about Sonship. But without the groundwork laid beforehand, I would not have entered into a new actuality. I see now how someone could leave that message and think, "Boy, that was anointed," yet not be changed. But for many years, there was a working of my heart prior to that message. That work turned my heart into receptive soil—well-fertilized, perfectly tilled and ready for the message to be delivered.

The messages of "Not I but Christ" and "Christ in you, the hope of glory" are received through impartation. And why does it have to be given through example, not just teaching? Because *Life* begets life. The reality of resurrected Life, which is *Christ's Life*, has to be transferred through a willing vessel of that Life. Someone has to carry the message and pay the price in this life for that message to be birthed in another.

> *We continually share in the death of Jesus in our own bodies so that the resurrection life of Jesus will be revealed through our humanity. We consider living to mean that we are constantly being handed over to death for Jesus' sake so that the life of Jesus will be revealed through our humanity.* ***So, then, death is at work in us but it releases life in you.***
>
> 2 Corinthians 4:10-12 TPT

Who will do this? Servants of the Lord, like Paul, who receive little thanks though they carry others within the womb of their own spirits to birth Christ's Life in them. Paul travailed with birth pangs until Christ was formed in the Galatians (Gal. 4:19). He gave evidence of the resurrected Life and carried sons full-term to birth. Paul's job was not primarily to stand up and explain the revelation; he had to live it out before them, transferring the Life of which he spoke. This is discipleship! It is the *making of disciples*.

The exchanged Life only comes through an exchange of lives.

What follows here is a transcript of excerpts from Art Katz's pivotal message, *Attaining to Sonship.* Full permission to include this amazing teaching has been granted by Art's daughter, Sissie Katz-Pennel, with Ben Israel Fellowship and Art Katz Ministries, and I am so grateful!

> "In the selection of May 28 from *My Utmost for His Highest*, Oswald Chambers has as his verse something from John chapter 16. *'And in that day you shall ask Me nothing.'* Maybe you want to turn to John 16. We cannot even conceive that there would be a day in which we need not ask the Lord anything. What does he mean by that?
>
> "Verse 23: *'And in that day you shall ask me nothing. Verily, verily, I say unto you, if ye shall ask anything of the Father, He will give it to you in My name. Hitherto have ye asked nothing in My name: ask, and ye shall receive, that your joy may be made full. These things have I spoken unto you in proverbs: but the time cometh, when I shall no more speak unto you in proverbs, but I shall show you plainly of the Father. At that day ye shall ask in My name: and I say not unto you, that I will pray the Father for you: For the Father Himself loveth you, because ye have loved Me, and have believed that I came out from God. I came forth from the Father, and am come into the world: again, I leave the world, and go to the Father.'* Verses 32 and 33: '*Behold, the hour cometh, yea, is now come, that ye shall be scattered, every man to his own, and shall leave Me alone. And yet I am not alone, because the Father is with Me. These things I*

have spoken unto you, that in Me ye might have peace. In the world ye shall have tribulation, but be of good cheer: I have overcome the world.'

"So Oswald Chambers asked, 'When is 'that day'? When the Ascended Lord makes you one with the Father. In that day you will be one with the Father as Jesus is, and 'in that day,' Jesus says, 'You shall ask Me nothing.'"

"Do you know why? Because the distinction between you and the Me whom you are asking is abolished. There's no you to ask. Because you have been taken up and subsumed into Him, there's no need to ask.

"Asking is only valid when you stand as an independent entity outside from God, asking Him for things that will enable you to perform for God. And that has been our characteristic mode until now. Which isn't bad. It's nice to receive from God grace and benefit and enablement and wisdom and the various things that make our service possible, but it's not the ultimate thing. There's a day. In that day, you'll ask Me nothing. And that day is the day in which we move from being the children of God to becoming the sons of God.

"We move from well-meaning and well-intending charismatic evangelicals to those who have come into union with God Himself. Where you cannot say where the believer ends and where the Lord begins. Have you the faith to believe for a union of that kind with God, which is nothing less and other than Jesus Himself enjoyed with the Father? I in Him and He in Me. This is not a play on words. It's too critical a subject merely to be a platform for fanciful language. It's graphic, it's accurate, it's literal that there is the possibility of a relationship with God the Father through Jesus of the very same kind that Jesus Himself enjoyed and exhibited.

"And that's how He could say, 'The words that I speak to you are not My words but the words that My Father has given Me.' He never did anything independent of the Father. He never had a thought, He never had any intention. Do you doubt that if He wanted to act out of His own personality and humanity He could've cut a pretty impressive swath? Don't you think He could've made quite an impressive display? But He was painstakingly consistent in His union with the Father that He would not even allow anything to rise out of His humanity but only that which He received of the Father.

"And yet the remarkable thing is that Jesus is in no way diminished by that relationship. He's not a mere automaton. He's not a little puppet being played upon by a greater power. The paradox is that in losing His life and not asserting His manhood, which was supreme, He through virtue of the union with the Father comes forth as the Son in all of the rich uniqueness that the word Son implies. In that day!"

"Until the ascension, resurrection Life of Jesus is manifested in you, you want to ask for this and that. Then after a while you find all the questions are gone. You do not seem to have any left to ask. You have come to a place of entire reliance and trust on the resurrection Life of Jesus. In fact, you can say 'in that day' with Paul, 'for me to live is Christ.'

"How many of us who are here this afternoon have ever said that? Or have just said it in a kind of hopeful, wishful way – how many of us can say it with the same kind of absolute confidence as Paul himself? Or do you think that Paul is something in himself apart from the Life and Resurrection of Jesus? Paul was nothing more or other than the continuation of that Life. And anything that Paul says or performs is anything and everything that the Lord Himself would have done had He yet been in His own body. Now He's in Paul.

"That's what makes an apostle an apostle. So, for us to celebrate Paul as Paul, to think what he's exhibiting is some unique Jewish character of courage or insight is to miss the point entirely. In Him, I believe Paul said, "I move and live and have my being." Now in the new Katz edition of the Bible, I would probably say, 'The Lord would say, 'In Paul, I move and live and have my being.' How do you like that? That the continuation of the Life of God in the Son Jesus, yet in His unfinished purposes, waits on a body that will allow Him to be the source of their life—their inspiration, their speaking, their ministry, their love, their wisdom, their understanding.

"But don't think that you're going to go boom! from where you are now to that, without passing through a no man's land of actual testing. Where you have no love, you have no wisdom, you have no power, you have no authority. You have voided, you have pulled out the plug of your own confidence in yourself. Where you're going to serve God if only He will give you help and the ability. And if there's no resurrection, you of all people are most to be pitied. And the Lord will test you. Because we are dead and hid with Christ in God until His life is revealed. And when it's revealed, it's revealed on to glory.

"But that doesn't mean when it's revealed it will come in the form that you will desire, enjoy, or appreciate. It may come in a form that makes you appear as a dumb-dumb. Where there is no cleverness, there is no brightness, you're without answer. In fact, you're surprisingly weak. You're dead and hid with Christ in God until His Life is revealed. But His Life is not revealed according to the terms of our desire, satisfaction, or need, but His. And it will take the form and the expression that He will be pleased to give it. And more often than not you will be humiliated both waiting for the expression of the Life and for the very expression itself. It's not going to necessarily make you bright. It may even make you lousy company. You may have even been a more charming, and more agreeable, and more impressive person when you operated under your own life then when you operate under His."

"But the condition for His Life is the forfeiting of your own. So, you're a dead man. You're dead and hidden with God and Christ until…. Not many people have the stomach for that. It takes a sublime confidence that Jesus was raised from the dead and because He lives, we shall live also.

"How many of us are the children of the Resurrection? Sons and daughters of the Resurrection is something more than the approval of the doctrine. And I can just say with complete safety and assurance, the overwhelming majority of Christians, even of a charismatic kind in the earth today, do not live out of the resurrection Life. They approve the doctrine, but they live out of themselves. Which is not a bad thing. I mean it can even be impressive from time to time and God will even give, in His grace, a little enablement. The only thing wrong with it is this: it falls short of His glory.

"And it requires not just a once and for all death but repeated deaths, like right now. I know I give the appearance of being self-assured as if I'm some kind of professional, and I can get up at will and open my mouth and it's all going to come out. If I'm not a dead man now, trusting God now, you may hear something clever, even biblical, even impressive, momentarily blessing, but it will not be Life-giving. This subject this afternoon is so crucially important for all the church in the last days, that no man however gifted or experienced is competent to deliver this word. It has got to be the manifestation of His Life because it is about His Life. Otherwise, it would be a contradiction of terms. That God should call you to the reality of His Life, that you might live in the power of His resurrection, by a man who is speaking out of his own humanity is a patent contradiction.

"The content has got to be in keeping with the mode. 'Well, Art, how come you don't sound like Jesus? I can pick up your Brooklyn accent. Don't tell me that's the life of God, Jesus doesn't have a Brooklyn accent.' That's how much you know. He'll have an accent of any kind that He Himself has imputed to that vessel. You think that my birth in Brooklyn is an accident and a happenstance? Or your birth, or your nationality, or origin, or formation, or personality is in any way just something God just has to make the best of? Or is it the explicit sovereign choosing of God whose Voice is the voice of many waters and brings forth the fullness of His counsel and His wisdom through the diversity of the vessels in whom His life operates and speaks.

"We mustn't be deceived that it's going to come out of some kind of sound chamber—"Thus saith the Lord." It will be very natural, it will be unaffected, but the origin is not out of man but out of God. And that man who is speaking has not chosen the subject for himself and has not, in himself, the ability to deliver it… But the life of Christ can. And the wisdom of Christ can meet their wisdom and reveal it as foolishness. If that were not so, any attempt to go speak would be foolhardy and vain.

"The only thing that justifies such a going is that the One who sends is also the One who goes with you and will be your life, your wisdom, your utterance, your sweetness of spirit, your charm, your severity, your authority, your everything required for life. 'He is your life' is the amplitude of everything that pertains to godliness and to life."

The Ultimate Reward of
The Great Exchange

The normal Christian life is the life of the Lord Jesus lived within the life of the believer. He is our abundant life.

Dr. V. Raymond Edman
(Minister, author, president of Wheaton College, 1900-1967)

A Mystery Revealed

"That they may all be one; even as You, Father, are in Me and I in You, that they also may be in Us, so that the world may believe that You sent Me."
John 17:21

There are moments in time that God reveals mysteries deep and unknown. He opens up His *Heart* for the purpose of showing us things about Himself. He says, "Call to Me, and I will answer you, and show you great and mighty things, which you do not know" (Jeremiah 33:3). Let me share with you just such a Heart-opening.

I know what Church is! I have the purpose of Church. Church is the Father loving the Son and the Son loving the Father in our own bodies—"That they will all be one, just as You and I are one."

The blessing of my finger being juiced off has been so amazing—addition not subtraction. During that episode, I saw that the Son of God came into a dark, worship-less place of my heart and *became* worship of the Father. I saw how the Son of the Living God took residence and ownership of a place of bondage in my life. I was fearful of death and illness, and Jesus entered that place and claimed it as His own. He did this by becoming one with the Father *in that place* and worshipping Him in it. Jesus worshipped where I had no worship.

It was an amazing thing to have this mystery performed within my frame, but now He is expanding the scope of my seeing. It actually goes beyond an individual expression to include Church. Yes, He showed me that this same interaction is supposed to be transpiring in His Church. And not only just *occurring* in His Church, but this actually ***IS*** true Church! Church is when the Father and the Son are one within the members of His Body. This is actual fellowship of the Godhead between individual members of His Body. Talk about true unity and union. Church is a circular living flow of fellowship and perfect agreement of the Godhead. It's LOVE and WORSHIP!

I agree to be indwelt by the love of the Father, and when I let Him love Christ in you, my brother and sister, and you receive it as the love of the Father for the Son, *then we are one!* In simple terms, Father-God is loving Christ in you, and Jesus is responding to the Father's love and loving Him in return. This is the embodiment of John 17:21. This is Church; everything else is just a civic organization.

"This worship wasn't for me nor was it about me, but it completely included me."

Oneness is literally Christ and the Father being one in our bodies. It is not agreement, proximity, corporate unity—no, it is oneness in HIM. Church is when we are made one ***in*** the oneness of Christ and the Father. Unhindered fellowship between the Godhead makes you and me…*Church*. Then you and I are connected with a bond that is so much higher than mere human connection. Our love becomes so much more radiant than frail, fickle human love. It becomes a tidal wave of Lordship, ownership, headship, union, and intimacy.

Imagine, I can literally be a vessel the Father uses to commune with His Son, and then we – His Body – can be the walking expression of *Their* union. And as it says in John 17:21, ***then*** the world will know that the Father sent the Son. True evangelism is being an indwelt vessel of the union of the Father and Son!

I understand (if understanding is even possible) that the union of the Trinity dwells in His earthen vessels to express the Son's love for the Father and the Father's love for the Son. Amazingly, this brings forth the Kingdom on earth and is *true Church*. It is a Holy reality and a complete mystery, in which I am so excited to be lost.

Bridal Preparation in The Great Exchange

The awe-inspiring part of the Great Exchange is Bridal preparation. Christ's Life as my life is my preparation for being His Bride. Love is volitional because loving someone is a choice. So, our weakness becomes another way for us to express our love and dependence on our Bridegroom.

You show your Beloved that you choose Him over yourself with each exchanged step. And even the struggle to do so is proof of the progress you make.

The daily choosing of Jesus over me is an expression of my love and forges our relationship as Bride and Bridegroom. Knowing that the crosses I face in this life are but Christ's preparation of me to be eternally His Bride is so encouraging. It helps me to embrace my crosses to know that Jesus is living His Life through me in them. The cross is always redemptive, not punitive, and without exception, the cross-life is for Bridal preparation.

Here is the truth: I cannot have Christ live His Life in me without facing my daily cross. It is the fire for the Refiner. By nature, light dispels darkness, and this will be my experience if I choose His Light over my darkness.

> *Let us rejoice and shout for joy! Let us give Him glory and honor, for the marriage of the Lamb has come [at last] and His bride (the redeemed) has prepared herself." She has been permitted to dress in fine linen, dazzling white and clean—for the fine linen signifies the righteous acts of the saints [the ethical conduct, personal integrity, moral courage, and godly character of believers].*
>
> Revelation 19:7-8 AMP

The Ultimate Purpose of it ALL

What is the purpose of Christ's Life as my life? Why this Great Exchange? It is not merely to save me from hell. It is not just that Christ wants to satisfy the requirements of the Law in me. And it is not simply so His Life could be manifested to the world. It also was not solely so that Jesus could bring the Father pleasure through my life. The main reason that the Father fashioned our lives to be about Christ's Life in our body is for UNION.

We were created and purposed for divine, intimate union with God. This is the goal of all things. God wants to be one with His created Bride and the exchanged Life is His flawless Way. Perfectly planned, exquisitely designed. God had a story that included our creation, fall, redemption and dependence unto union. He would be ONE with the one He loved. UNION was His intended goal all along! You cannot be any closer than to be ONE. Union is perfection and divine.

Everything in the world is set to oppose this divine union. False union is offered through many counterfeits, some purporting to be 'good.' Familial union, marital union, sexual union, unity of the church, a union through purpose…all are substitutes of the one *true* UNION which is Christ's Life as my life. I experience union as He lives in me, *as me*.

Though the assault against our union is great, the Solution is clear. Once more:

Christ's life as my life
is His Life in my life,
and that's not my life as His Life,
it's HIM.

In finding the Solution, we will find the One who is our answer. Jesus answers me through being me. He solves my quandary within Himself. The answer to how I can live this life is resolved *by Him living it*. Far more than just a how-to, Christ becomes my eternal answer in UNION.

We were crafted, formed, and designed for one purpose: UNION. Not work, not effort, not producing, not service…**UNION**.

What does this union look like? How does it manifest?

One crisp spring day, I was slowly driving through the North Georgia mountains, windows all down, and I just marveled at the beautiful, rolling green hills and lush fields of newly sprouted, green grass. In that moment, I was hit with the reality that Jesus Christ was looking through my eyes. That He was gazing upon His creation through them. Jesus was looking at *His* property and using my eyes to do it. I was the vessel for Him to take in the lay of that particular land.

But not just for Him. Jesus wanted to view this land *through* me. He wanted to see it through my eyes, as me. Unlike picking up a standard set of glasses, viewing the world through me flavors the scene. The view is completely unique because of my individual purview. Jesus wanted to see things my way – through *my eyes – through my life*. We viewed the scene *together*.

I felt Jesus' presence behind my eyes *like heat*, and all I could do was weep. What an awesome privilege to be the vessel He used to view His own lovely handiwork!

God indwells us to touch His world about us. When we live in the resurrected life, we are no longer living in and for ourselves; we are simply in Him. Then it is He touching our earth from heaven through our bodies. We are seated with Him in heaven, and now it is His touch, His sight, His smell, His tasting, and His hearing all through us, *as us*, in Him.

This is one of those difficult realities in which to have faith. "It's Him and not me?! But I feel so alive!" Jesus says that for me to live is Christ, so *it's not I*. This pushes every doubt-button in my body, but the Word says it, so it must be true. The crucified life is a life *free from self* and filled with Christ.

The reason for this is that Christ in me increases His Kingdom in the world. Though He does not *need* me, I am a vessel He uniquely created. *We are in union.* All of my work and effort has never amassed anything good, but Christ's Life in me brings His rule and reign into my world daily.

I have been crucified with Christ. ***It is no longer I who live, but Christ who lives in me.*** *And the life I now live in the flesh I live by faith in the Son of God, who loved me and gave Himself for me.*
Gal 2:20 ESV

For to me, to live ***is Christ*** *and to die is gain.*
Philippians 1:21 NASB

For you have died and ***your life is hidden with Christ in God****.*
When Christ, ***who is your life****, appears, then you also will appear with Him in glory.*
Colossians 3:4

From Now to Eternity
The Great Exchange

Christ's Life as my life is union unlike any other. I see Christ walk this earth, *now*, in my living reality. I witness His revealing in my world and to those I encounter. There is no greater gift for those I love than to give them Jesus *through me*.

People talk about impacting the world *for* Christ. How about impacting your world *with* Christ? You get to witness Him live your life and love your world. It is a great privilege that we can both receive from others and give as well. Jesus paid a high price to enable this divine union, and to encounter Him requires but a YES.

The Great Exchange is the greatest of all living experiences… It is the mystery of the Gospel.

My Eternity
by Horatius Bonar

Upon a life I did not live,
upon a death I did not die;
Another's life, Another's death,
I stake my whole eternity.[5]

5 From a hymn written by Horatius Bonar in 1881 a Scottish minister and psalmist.

The Sovereign Touch

God is Either Sovereign Over All or He Isn't Sovereign at All.

Want to read more from John Enslow?

Want to read more from John Enslow?

GET ALONG WITH GOD

A blog about discovering a God worth knowing.

GetAlongWithGod.com

Check out our weekly podcast.

Available online at
www.shulamitepodcast.com
or through iTunes.

Shulamite Ministries

READMK.COM
Read articles, daily devotions and more on the Online Library of Martha Kilpatrick.

SHULAMITEPODCAST.COM
Listen to the weekly Shulamite Podcast, and hear unfiltered conversations about real life with Jesus.

GETALONGWITHGOD.COM
Interested in the ups and downs of discipleship? A blog about discovering a God worth knowing.

LIVINGCHRISTIANBOOKS.COM
Shop for all things Martha Kilpatrick as well as timeless classics by those who've gone before.

THE SHULAMITE APP
Tap into all the resources of Shulamite Ministries while on-the-go with your iPhone and iPad.

Easy to use and mobile-friendly, Shulamite.com houses our ministry's latest podcasts, daily devotions, blog posts and more. Stay up-to-date on ministry news, new teachings by Martha, and all upcoming events by making Shulamite.com a daily stop!

Here is a hub for the prodigals and the truth-seekers, the brokenhearted and the hungry—all who would discover a God worth knowing!